Couch Rebels

Because Stories Like These Aren't Told by Potatoes

Crowd-published for **impact** at CausePub.com

This book helps to provide clean water to communities
in Africa through BloodWaterMission.org

CAUSE/PUB

This publication is designed to provide competent and reliable information regarding the subject matter covered. However, it is sold with the understanding that the authors and publisher are not engaged in rendering legal, financial, or other professional advice. Law and practices often vary from state to state, and if expert assistance is required, the services of a professional should be sought. The authors and publisher specifically disclaim any liability that is incurred from the use or application of the contents of this book.

CausePub LLC
P.O. Box 63914
Colorado Springs, CO 80926

First ebook edition: August 2013
First print book edition: September 2013

The publisher is not responsible for websites (or their content) mentioned in this book that are not owned by the publisher.

To learn more about CausePub and how to get involved in the next book project, visit CausePub.com or Twitter.com/CausePub.

ISBN 978-0-9898139-1-4

Thank You!

A special thanks to everyone who made this book possible:

- To every author who submitted a story.
- To Beck Gambill and Marc Sandin for proofreading.
- To every person who clicked "like", tweeted #couchrebels, and told their friends how to get involved.
- To everyone who bought a copy of the book.
- To Blood:Water Mission for allowing us to partner with their incredible organization.

Your enthusiasm and support made it happen!

Thank you!

The CausePub Team

Table of Contents

Bloons Tower Defense
(The story behind the stories)

"How you doin'?" I asked as I crawled into bed.

"Doing OK," replied Michelle. "I just got a Super Monkey and a Fire Ring, but I need help. Here, you play."

"Oh, dang!" I exclaimed as I took the Macbook from her. "You're on round 59 already! 63 is coming soon - we need more Moab Maulers at the front of the track."

"I know, I know. But the first ten rounds were really tough and I wasn't able to buy a Banana Farm soon enough," she said shamefully.

"Oh well. Even if we lose this game, it's only 11:05 PM. We can start another one."

I grew up despising 98% of all video games. There were a few that would monopolize my time and attention during certain winter seasons (Sim City, Sim Tower, and 007 for N64), but for the most part I was obsessed with building forts, playing soccer and chopping down trees (to build more forts).

Now here I am, a 29 year old dad, staying up late on weeknights playing a game where the sole objective is to pop balloons.

Digital balloons.
Pink, black, and even zebra colored digital balloons.

Pathetic?
Almost.

Ninja Kiwi's *Bloons Tower Defense* really *is* an addicting game -
at least for my wife and me. I can't begin to add up the number of
hours we've spent conquering all the different tracks. It's fun and
Michelle even considers it to be part of our "quality time"
together, so I'm not going to sit here and knock our favorite
game or even those times we've spent watching our favorite
prime-time shows (I feel no guilt over watching *Castle* every
week!).

We all need downtime. We all need to turn the brain off for a bit.

For a bit.

But.

But when it got to be 12:35 AM and we were still popping
balloons, I was forced to admit that our game-playing had
become an obsession and had moved far beyond moderation.

Is this really the richest use of our time together?

I started to reflect. I realized that the rich times in my life were
often defined by experiences off the couch.

   - Helping my dad clean out the garage and install a

sprinkler system in our backyard taught me how to work hard.

- Re-dedicating my life to Christ and experiencing the presence of the Holy Spirit for the first time while on a middle school retreat began my personal relationship with my Savior.

- Traveling to Zambia on a mission trip with one friend and 70 other South Africans I'd never met, broadened my worldview and sparked a fire for leaving an impact on those in need.

- Marrying my wife and witnessing the births of my two daughters showed me what true humility and dependence really are.

- Hiring a homeless guy who needed work gave me the opportunity to join what the Lord was already doing in His heart.

- Singing my daughters to sleep every night (despite how tired I am) gives me a special bond with them and an open door for investing in their character.

These are all experiences that have left a huge impact on who I am today. They all involve taking action and getting off the couch (whether that's by me or someone else). If my dad hadn't gotten off his couch, I might be a lazy fool. If the speaker at the retreat hadn't gotten off his couch, I may not have ever known Jesus like I know Him today. If I hadn't gotten off my couch and proposed to my wife, I'd be single, daughterless, and a freaking idiot.

To me, the couch is a zone of complacency. Complacency is attractive. It's comfortable.

But is it really?

Is anyone *really* comfortable living life on the sidelines?

I had a theory. The theory was, as my good friend Doug often says, "two-fold".

> #1: There is a deep hunger in every single one of us to experience life off the couch more than we currently do.

> #2: We're all scared to get off the couch, but we're all inspired to do so when we see others doing it.

On April 1st, 2013, Ken Norwood and I launched CausePub and started collecting Couch Rebel stories. By July 20th we had collected 155 stories from 127 different authors.

I was blown away.

On Aug 3rd, I announced that 86 of those stories were going to be published in this book.

A few days before that, I had contacted the five authors who had the most votes for their stories. The idea was to come up with a marketing strategy for selling this book based on methods that had already worked for those top-voted authors.

The question was simple. "How did you get the word out about your story?"

Lori Harris, author of the story *When Your People and Your Place Happens to be Your Hometown*, replied back immediately. She started off telling me that she and her husband had recently moved back to a small city in NC called Rocky Mount. She was originally from there but had escaped in 2003 because it was and is extremely corrupt.

She informed me, "...our city is often topping the charts for all the wrong reasons- crime, job loss, education, housing market, drug abuse, and rampant dealing. I could go on."

And then she told me something totally unexpected.

> "Let me be very honest, I chose to write my story because your prompt was easy for me. I am living as a missionary in my hometown. I blog and have developed a small following (only about 350) and in recent months, the majority of my readers appear to live in Rocky Mount. I think I got so many votes because I was able to rally my city to come together for something positive instead of something negative. Our city needed a win, a prettier dot on the map, and I believe they wanted to see a good story come from Rocky Mount and so they did their part in voting and talking about CausePub.

> "In the last 2 weeks, as my email box filled with other locals telling their stories, I was inspired to compile their stories on a blog for our city. [Couch Rebels] has inspired our small town to live missionally, seek the good, find God where He is at work, and join Him here, in Rocky Mount."

No longer was my theory just a theory.

I hope that you read these stories with a rebellious attitude. You don't need to stop popping *Bloons* altogether, but as you read, I hope you'll be inspired to pop a little bit less.

I know *I* am.

Here's to changing the world through stories,

Author: Griff Hanning

Founder of CausePub and instigator of this Couch Rebels project. Obsessed with my family, Jesus, and new ideas. Let's make an impact together!

CausePub.com

The Starbucks Neighbor

I made my way through the large glass doors that marked the entrance to our hotel on Fisherman's Wharf, and had to pause.

The crisp early morning air rushed to embrace me like a long-lost friend. Shrouded in a dense fog, it's touch awoke my senses.

My eyes traveled longingly across the street to the Bay. Past the Hyde Street Pier, the Golden Gate Bridge played a game of peek-a-boo through the mist, teasing me with faint glimpses of its famous red hue. Not far from this architectural marvel, the eerie shadow of the retired penitentiary on the island of Alcatraz was a stoic watchman. Its now-empty cells guarding nothing but memories.

I inhaled deeply, savoring the salty sea air and the unmistakable aroma of fresh seafood -- rock crab, bay shrimp, California halibut. The tang of sourdough bread drifted down Jefferson Street from Boudin's Bakery.

A slight drizzle misted my hair as I turned the corner. Leaving Jefferson I continued up Hyde.

Pulling my white jacket snugly around me I had to smile at the sight of the Hyde-Powell cable car turnaround. Historic Ghirardelli Square served as its backdrop standing one block west.

It was surreal.

For years I had wanted to visit San Francisco. After much

wishing, finally, I was here.

And on this Saturday morning, as my husband Ted enjoyed the luxury of sleeping in, I ventured out for coffee.

Rounding the corner to Starbucks, the perfect in my morning came to a screeching halt at the sight of a large, hunched over form.

I hesitated, my defenses rising. It was either forge on ahead, coffee still my goal, or turn back and avoid what I knew was coming -- a request for money.

The desire for coffee won. With my uncertainty somewhat in check, I put one foot in front of the other.

Two steps later, it came.

"Help a homeless woman?"

I glanced down. A large green comforter adorned her shoulders, under it a floral blanket like the ones I remember using at my grandparents' house as a kid. Both kept watch against the early morning chill. Next to her sat plastic grocery bags, each home to a handful of aluminum cans on their way to recycling.

Uncomfortably, I replied, "No."

I quickly climbed the small staircase to Starbucks. Taking two steps at a time, I put into practice what Lot's wife lacked the self-control to carry out: I didn't look back.

Inside, I worked to quiet my racing heart.

Since our arrival in San Francisco, homeless people had become a familiar sight. I'd grown accustomed to being asked for money. Sometimes by those living on the streets. Other times by individuals peddling maps who sought to profit from our wonder-filled expressions, which clearly marked us as tourists.

Up until now, Ted stood at my side, offering a sense of security. Today, on my own, I felt unprotected and insecure.

"One tall, peppermint mocha frappuccino," I told the barista, deciding to play it safe and go with a slight twist on one of my favorites.

Standing there, the bananas on the counter caught my eye. It was then that my resolve broke. I looked back.

"Jesus," my heart whispered, "what would He do?"

In that moment, a story he told to a lawyer two thousand years ago became my own.

"A man was going down from Jerusalem to Jericho and he fell among robbers, who stripped him and beat him and departed, leaving him half dead" (Luke 10:30, ESV).

I knew little about the woman outside. And in all honesty, had my doubts as to whether she was homeless. But there was one thing I didn't doubt -- that she had been battered and beaten by the harshness of life and the realities of sin. Like me, she had need of a Savior.

15

"Now by chance a priest was going down that road, and when he saw him he passed by on the other side. So likewise a Levite, when he came to the place and saw him, passed by on the other side" (Luke 10:31-32).

When the priest and the Levite spotted the man on the road, they didn't know what brought him there. Was he a drunk? Had a series of poor decisions finally landed him rock bottom? Perhaps his wounds were self-inflicted.

I, too, had questions.

What compelled this woman to sit on a San Francisco street corner and beg? Had she fallen on hard times, and like the well-known story of Christopher Gardner in "The Pursuit of Happyness," unexpectedly found herself homeless? Or, were the doubts I harbored legitimate?

Like the priest and the Levite, I allowed my questions to justify passing by a broken individual, afraid to become involved even by the small act of offering pocket change. My love for God took second place to my fear.

"But a Samaritan, as he journeyed, came to where he was, and when he saw him, he had compassion. He went to him and bound up his wounds, pouring on oil and wine. Then he set him on his own animal and brought him to an inn and took care of him" (Luke 10:33-34).

As the Samaritan, was I willing to move past apprehension and show compassion regardless of what her story was? Or would I leave that to other early morning coffee drinkers?

Wrestling with these questions, my brown boots didn't seem that different from the worn, dust-covered sandals of the ancient lawyer. My heart, as his, was seeking to justify myself. "Who is my neighbor?" I asked silently, hoping that Jesus *wouldn't* point to the homeless woman outside.

But He did.

In the end, I faced a question much like the lawyer did, "Who, do you think, proved to be a neighbor to the woman begging on a San Francisco street corner?"

Silently, I echoed the lawyer: "The one who showed mercy.

"Anything else?" the barista asked.

"Yes, one drip coffee and a banana," I replied. "It's for my neighbor."

Author: Ashleigh Slater

Ashleigh Slater is a freelance writer and editor who writes regularly for Ungrind.org, Start Marriage Right, and iBelieve.com. She lives in Atlanta, Georgia, with her husband Ted and four daughters.

Ashleighslater.com

When Your People and Your Place Happens to be Your Hometown

She stands next to the ironing board, iron in hand, my husband's button down in the other and I watch her as she flings the iron back and forth in the air, steam rising from the heat of the water.

She's talking a blue streak and she's making no good sense, when she says, "I'm bipolar, you know. You care if I go smoke one on your porch?"

"Sure. Go ahead," I say, hoping the cigarette will calm her down. I watch as she digs into her bag and I can't help but think God made a mistake in sending me here.

I'd rather give her a twenty and do the ironing myself than spend the afternoon giving her a job.

I can't help this girl, and frankly, I don't want to.

The kids are on the porch swing waiting for us when we pull into the drive. All three of them, shoeless, coatless, and covered in grime.

They scratch their heads because the lice won't leave them alone; I scratch my own head, grimacing inwardly at the thought of lice.

I park the car and watch as my small tribe tumbles out to welcome their friends.
I inwardly groan because I'm tired and I'm worn and my heart is too small to care for three more kids. Especially kids with lice.

I got nothing, Lord...

I step over bits of glass and beer cans and make my way to the front door, silently praying no one is home.

A stench permeates the air surrounding the door and I realize that there really is no front door. It is simply a door frame covered in scraps of fabric, each scrap covering a square where a piece of glass should have been.

I knock on the side of the house, next to the door, and I mentally prepare myself for a face to appear.

"Hello. I live just a few doors down and I wanted to bless you with a loaf of bread because Jesus is the bread of life. Is there a specific way that I can ask Jesus to bless you this week?"

I run the words over and over again in my head, and relief washes over me when no one comes to the door.

I leave the loaf of bread on the porch and I escape the moment.

And all I can think about is how this family needs more than a loaf of bread.

And I don't have more.

It's early evening when I find a minute to myself. The sunlight lingers over the yard as I watch the children play ball on the lawn.

My legs dangle from the porch swing and I absentmindedly read a paperback. A glass of wine warms in my hand.

"Hey. Is the preacher home?" Startled at the suddenly nearby voice, I look up in time to see him stride across the road. He's dressed like he's been at the restaurant, his white jacket smeared with grease, which reeks of seafood as he comes closer.

"Hi Dennis. No, he's not home yet. He's watering the grass at the warehouse. I'll tell him you stopped by, though." I pause, waiting for him to wave and move on to wherever he is headed. He just stands there, looking at me, like he has nowhere to go.

"So how's Jade?" I ask. "Have you seen her lately? Do you still get supervised visits?"
He sits on the edge of the porch and I shift on the swing, knowing I've just given him a reason to stay.

I exhale and I silently pray, "Help me Jesus."

Three years have now passed since God gave us a people and a place.

We've only lived here, in this place, for 19 short months.

And I've only recently begun to open my heart up to these people.

We live in Small Town, North Carolina, smack dab between the railroad tracks and tobacco fields…

A place where racial tension runs deep and wide,
A place where the have-nots far outnumber the haves,
A place where gangs clamor for territory and drugs run rampant,
A place where farmers still farm and families still live on family
homesteads,
And a place where almost everyone goes to church but few
really seem to know Christ.
This place is my hometown, the very place that made me.

I've spent half of my life living on the outskirts of this city, sitting
under a steeple, avoiding the very people I now call neighbors.
Most days, I find that I still try to avoid the ragamuffins around
the corner…until I remember that I am one of them.

And on those days, those days when I roll out of bed and find
myself standing neck deep in grace, I make Koolaid and serve
cookies to those filthy kids on my front porch.
I open wide my home and my hands…

And I crack open my heart just a little bit more.

I smile now, even as I write this, because God is up to *something*
here, and I've just realized His *something* might just be
something in me.

Author: Lori Harris

Wife to a church planter in Small Town, NC. Mother of six. Mess of a woman. Lover of authentic community. Wild JOY seeker. Some days a blogger, most days a journaler. Always prone to wander.

LoriHarris.me

27 Flies

It was hard to breathe. We had turned off the fan in the corner so the rattling wouldn't be heard in the video we were about to shoot. The moment we switched it off the air grew heavy and thick. Flies buzzed around our heads. The men all clutched handkerchiefs, wiping the sheen of sweat off of their faces every few minutes. Sweat formed at my temples and brow, dripping into my eyes.

We were in a dusty corner of West Africa, gathering stories for the non-profit organization I worked for. I would fill a red-dirt stained notebook with facts and details and quotes, and then spin those messy notes into stories on the plane ride home. And then hopefully... *hopefully* someone sitting in their living room in the prosperous United States would read my words and those stories would prod and poke them to action with the needle of conviction.

But writing was the easy part. The hard part was sitting in this tiny living room in Africa and teasing the story from the thick, chewable air.

The father who sat before me quietly answered our questions. He told us about leaving their home at 5:30 in the morning to go to his job as a driver. How he spent half of his salary each month on the rent of this 10×10 concrete room. How he could only pay for food one week a month, charging the rest.

And then he told us about his wife. Visibly, he shrank before my eyes. He told us about her death five years ago. His shoulders slumped. He stared at the ground. His voice was so quiet, I had to lean forward. More flies flew in through the open door.

His heartbreak was a presence in the room. It was heavier than the heat. It settled over us. A knot the size of the limes growing on the trees in the front yard formed in my throat.

My eyes darted around the room. I so badly wanted a distraction. It was too much. So I began to count the flies that crawled on our arms as he choked on the memories of his wife.

1, 2, 3…

She had been walking home with their 8-year-old daughter.

4, 5, 6, 7…

Screeching tires, a spray of dust and gravel.

8, 9, 10, 11, 12…

So quickly, as only a mother can react, she shoved her child aside, a tumble of bright fabric and red dirt.

13, 14, 15, 16…

And then, she was gone. Instantly, her husband became a single father, raising four children, including a one-month-old son.

17, 18, 19, 20, 21, 22…

He had never remarried. The grief was too deep. The responsibility too great. The loss too profound.

23, 24, 25, 26, 27.

"She left me," he whispered.

I looked up at those words, and stared into a face that had seen too much. I wanted to touch his arm. Tell him that it would be okay. But we were all frozen in place. So I simply reached out and swept my arm through the humid air, scattering the 27 flies.

They buzzed in the air, joining the heat and the grief. I waved my arm again, shooing them towards the door. A few flew out. I waved harder, trying to clear the air, but knowing the cloud that hung there was not composed of flies.

And no amount of arm waving I could do today would bring relief to the broken man sitting before me.

Author: Brandy Campbell

I am a writer, reader, baker, listener, laugher. A daughter, sister, friend. I like old books, new friends, quilts, coffee. I hate running, indigestion, slimy okra. I want to forgive, love, feel, be.

BrandyCampbell.com

Fearing Fatherhood

For most of my childhood I had a frightening hunch that I would one day be a dad. Why was my hunch frightening? Because I was raised by a single-mother. What did I know about being a dad? One day my kid would ask me questions that every dad knows how to answer. Every dad but me.

"Dad, how do you clean a fish?"

"Just cut his head off, son. The rest should take care of itself from there."

"Dad, what does a spark plug do?"

"Hey look, a butterfly."

My senior year of high school I failed out of a trigonometry class and got put in a wood shop class. This excited me. Trigonometry didn't seem to have a lot to offer but wood shop would probably help me to learn some dad things. This way, if my kid ever asked me what a spark plug did, I could at least build him a bird house. My first few days in wood shop were spent telling jokes and seeing who could hammer a nail into a board the fastest.

And then, almost as quickly as it started, I got taken out of that wood shop class. I don't think anyone else, in the history of public education, has ever been taken out of wood shop. Wood shop classes exist for the kids that get taken out of other classes. When school administrators pull you from a wood shop class, it's sort of like getting kicked out of prison. My fears of fatherhood remained.

So, I got put in an electronics class. I was okay with this. Now, whenever my kid would ask me what a spark plug does I could teach him how to slide his church shoes on the carpet and electrocute his friends. That's classic dad stuff, right? Unfortunately, all we ever did in electronics class was watch movies. The movie we watched the most was Short Circuit starring Steve Guttenberg. The good news is that I got an A in that class. The bad news is that now, whenever my kids ask me what a spark plug does, I tell them a stupid joke and talk about the Police Academy movies.

I'm a 37-year-old father of two young boys, and my worst fears have finally been realized. I don't know a lot of dad stuff, and I think my kids are on to me. My oldest son wants to build a tree house. I'm really hoping Jesus comes back before that time comes.

To compensate for my lack of knowledge I try to spend a lot of time with my boys doing what I did as a kid: playing outside, playing on the floor, praying, reading the Bible, loving mom and watching Kung Fu Theater. Sadly, Kung Fu Theater doesn't come on anymore but there are worthy substitutes.

I always pick up my youngest son, kiss him and ask him who he loves. He's 16 and really hates when I do this. Seriously, though... He's much younger than that, and every time I ask him who he loves he does the same thing. He points at the wall, or the ceiling, or the refrigerator. Anything but dad.

One day I was asking my son this question and he was giving his usual response when his older brother walked up and said, "Hey dad, ask me who I love."

I sensed a Hallmark moment coming so I gladly played along.

"Who do you love more than anybody in the whole world?"

"Mom!"

For a minute I felt like a real loser. I should have petitioned to stay in that wood shop class. But then it hit me.

Maybe my son loves his mom so much because he sees how much I love her. And maybe he'll grow to love Jesus even more because of how much I love Jesus. In a way that's kind of intimidating, but also, strangely, very liberating. Who cares if I don't know how to do a lot of dad stuff? If I can just, by God's grace, love my wife like Christ loves the church (Ephesians 5:25), train up my boys in the discipline and instruction of the Lord (Ephesians 6:4) and love Jesus more than anything else (Deuteronomy 6:5), I think all of the rest will be just fine.

This week I spent some time with a senior adult in my church. She lives alone and she says her kids are always asking her if she gets lonely in that big house all by herself. She tells them that she never gets lonely because she's never alone. And then she told me about the time a tornado came through her town in the 1930s and how her dad did a great job taking care of the family. The loving presence of her earthly father taught her a great lesson about the far greater loving presence of her heavenly Father.

I hope I teach the same lesson to my boys.

Author: Jay Sanders

I am the husband of one and the father of two. I am currently serving as the pastor of Towaliga Baptist Church in Jackson, Georgia.

Jasonlsanders.com

The First Time I Touched Poverty

In 2002 I went to Guadalajara on a five-day mission trip. I was amazed by many things, but Garbage City is what changed my life.

I thought John was exaggerating when he called it Garbage City. I had never imagined in my most desperate nightmares that I would ever see what I saw that day.

I don't know much Spanish, but I knew we had just entered a landfill. The towering heaps of trash seemed to stretch to the sky. And the stench was overpowering. But I was still confused why we were here.

"John, did you say we are going to minister to kids? Where are they?"

"Just wait a few minutes Chris, and you will understand."

We turned left and drove another five minutes. Another right turn. Another few hundred feet. Another left.

Then my heart broke.

On the corner of the street was what I can only describe as a lean-to, made entirely of garbage. A refrigerator door turned on its side formed the base of a wall, with a myriad of boxes and refuse heaped on top. A large cardboard box was the roof. The other wall was just junk. There was no door.

A woman, probably sixty years old, was shuffling along the road with a deep limp. When she saw our cars she smiled a toothless grin and hobbled more quickly. She shouted in Spanish down the road, to nobody it seemed.

Within thirty seconds we had to stop our vehicles. We were surrounded by children of all ages. Giggles and laughter and smiles on every single kid, even though their clothes wouldn't even qualify as rags in our country.

I started to cry, right there in the car. John placed a strong hand on my shoulder. "Welcome to Garbage City, Chris. This is what it means to be poor. Time to get out and show Jesus. Come on!"

John got out first. "Hola!" He shouted the greeting and opened his arms wide.

"Hola!" The crowd of children shouted back. Three kids were already climbing on John: one on his left arm, another on his legs, and a third climbing on his back. I held back in the car for a moment, paralyzed by fear.

What if I have nothing to offer these kids? What if they don't like me? What do I say, since we can't talk? What if they get me sick?

The last question brought me up short. *What if they get me sick?* My own selfishness punched me in the gut and took my breath away. I traveled all the way to Guadalajara to share the message of Jesus, and sat here, stifled by fear of illness. Lord, forgive me, I prayed as I opened the car door.

I was enveloped by kids large and small as soon as I got out. I am 6'7", and at once became a massive curiosity, like a sideshow circus attraction. We laughed. We played. We connected. Without needing a common spoken language.

John gathered the crowd of children and we gave out groceries for every family. Enough for a few days at least. Then we sang a few worship songs with the kids in Spanish. John shared a simple Gospel message and was met with a surprise. The shuffling old lady raised her hand and accepted Jesus that day. She told John her heart found healing because we played with the children, rather than shying away from their filth. We showed her Jesus she said.

My heart was forever changed by Garbage City. I still struggle with selfishness, but it's different. I know what real poverty looks like, and I know the power of investing in people's lives, even if they are literally filthy. Everyone is created in the image of God, and worth loving, not just those who dress like me, look like me, and live in the same tax bracket as me.

Once I held back in comfort and pride in my own world; now I can take love to people who can't meet me where I live, but who *can* receive it when I take it to them.

Author: Chris Morris

I am a CPA by day, but a creator at heart. I love telling stories to inspire and encourage people to keep hope in this busted world. I also love a great cup of French press coffee.

Chrismorriswrites.com

When You Want to Go, But You're Called to Stay

I'd pack my bag in a heartbeat, jump on a plane, and serve wherever He called me to. Sometimes I wish He would call me. I wish Jesus would whisper, "Go!" and I could take off and do the big things I dream.

Jesus hasn't called me to go. He's called me to stay right here. Jesus is asking me to live the life of a stay-at-home mom.

I'm not sure there's a place where I could feel more like I accomplish nothing. Three little ones clutch at me all day begging for something. The laundry, the clean dishes, the vacuuming, the cleaning of little hand prints and crayons off the wall, it's all undone by the time my husband walks in the door to see my look of complete desperation. I'm lucky; my husband has never once asked me "What did you *do* all day?"

By the time the three rascals (3 years and under) are tucked into bed, I have nothing left to give. Sometimes I despair that no one sees the work I do, that my work is not measurable, or that it's not as good as those missionaries that left everything they know to serve God. I wonder if God could use me at all.

One of my little girls has a strong will. (She may or may not have inherited it from her mother.) Disciplining this child is like wrestling with a hippopotamus. I remember one day when

she disobeyed. I don't remember the offense, but I do remember she began to kick and flail as I held her, firmly and gently, on the edge of my bed.

"I love you, sweet girl. I'm not hurting you. I love you enough to deal with your heart. I love you."

She was flailing, screaming, and chanting intermittently. "Mama, hurt me! No 'douch' me. No, snuggle me! Mama! Hurt me!"

All of a sudden I felt warm liquid oozing over my legs; I slid us quickly down to the floor.

For thirty minutes I sat in the urine, I rocked her, and I waited for her to wear herself out. I waited for her to come to the end of herself and accept that the correction I was giving her was what she needed. Then, I began to weep.

Am I not just like my daughter, kicking and screaming violently "Let me go!" rather than accepting that Jesus has asked me to be here? Do I not scoff at the job he asks me to do, disobeying in attitude, because I feel like this mothering task is so mundane?

I want to go somewhere and do something great for Christ so badly that I often reject the incredibly large calling He has given me here and now. Three little sinners live under my roof and look up to me (the more experienced one) all day long. They watch me sin, repent, and thank Jesus for his grace. I am the gospel walking and breathing grace into a tiny mission field.

The "mundane" calling of motherhood is so holy that it found me weeping and holding a little girl whose heart rebels just like mine, all while rancid pee dried stickily on my legs.

Eventually my little one relented. She accepted her punishment. I whispered to her how Jesus took the worst punishment of all for our disobedience so that we may enjoy His love forever. We hosed off our sticky legs and dried our tear streaked faces. She asked to sit in my lap while we ate lunch.

Maybe I have gotten this whole thing backward. Maybe motherhood is a calling worthy of praise. A calling of steadfast devotion to the little ones whose hearts need the gospel most of all.

Maybe, just maybe, staying and serving right in the midst of the motherhood mess is the place where grace can flow through me to the ends of the world.

Author: Melissa Aldrich

I rarely have it all together, but I know the One who does. Wife, Mother, photographer, writer. I encourage others (but mostly myself) to see the mess of daily life as real beautiful grace.

QuietGraces.com

My Sunshine

The old man had a wrinkled face and despondent eyes.

He was curled up into a little half ball, peering at us with quiet curiosity. His wife sat next to him, holding his hand, a thin sweater pulled over her skinny shoulders. There were no monitors to beep in the background. Only a skinny window with sunshine falling through and an empty IV pole.

We stood there, two American girls in a small Tongan hospital. Because we didn't speak the language, there was nothing we could say. A smile wasn't enough, that was clear. Not for this desperate man.

Frantic to impart something of worth to him, I wracked my twenty-year-old brain. What could we do? We were alone, Annie and I. The rest of our small pack of nursing students were lying by the hotel pool, soaking up the Tongan sunshine to take home an island tan. Instead of joining them for our block of free time, we had asked the front desk of the hotel for two black garbage bags and picked up litter along the beach.

Palangis. I thought I heard the old woman whisper to her husband. Yes, we were palangi's. White girls. The Tongans yelled it out their car window as they drove by us, honking.

Palangi!

It wasn't an insult, just a reminder. We weren't from here. But that didn't matter: we were here to help, to teach, to give. So that's what we did.

Once Annie and I had combed the nearest beach, we ditched the garbage bags into a communal trash can and wandered farther into the heart of the small island. The hospital seemed to find us.

And now we faced the old man and had nothing to say. Nurses walked back and forth in the hallways. They wore an all white uniform, complete with skirts and folded paper hats. It was like stepping into a history book.

His wife gave us a timid smile. She had a single braid in her hair, age lines around her brown face, and kind eyes. It was clear they felt as awkward as we did. The old man nodded to us once in greeting, making a soft swishing sound on the pillow as his head moved.

I turned to Annie.

"Let's sing something," I whispered. Music was universal. They wouldn't have to understand the words to know what we meant. She looked back in surprise.

"Like what?"

The old man and I locked eyes. His were chocolate brown, and tired.

"You Are My Sunshine," I said.

Annie's eyes lit up. "Perfect."

"You are my sunshine,

My only sunshine,"

The old mans lips curled into a slow smile when we started to sing, as if he recognized the song. The stressed look on the old woman's face receded a little.

"You make me happy
When skies are gray"

His pained eyes began to sparkle. He relaxed a little more into the frail pillow beneath him and looked between the two of us. The tip of my nose and my fingertips began to tingle. The old woman blinked several times.

"You'll never know dear
How much I love you.

Please don't take my sunshine away."

Annie's voice began to crack at the same time mine did. My vision was watery as we went into the second verse. Despite the drab walls, the feeling of sadness, and the uncertainty that hung in the air like curtains, I felt a light begin to fill up my heart.

This is what I'm here for, I thought. Not to get a tan next to a pool in my free time. We came on a humanitarian mission to connect with humans. Whether or not we speak his language, this man knows what we mean.

A heavy lump formed in the back of my throat as we neared the end of the song. The old man lifted a bony hand to his lips and pressed a kiss to it. When we finished the chorus, he sent the kiss to us.

We returned his smile through our tears.

Please don't take my sunshine away.

Author: Katie Cross

I'm a writer, a runner-spinner-weight lifter, a vizsla mama, a husband-obsessor, a nurse and a girl that really likes to eat cookies.

kcrosswriting.com

The Miles I Have Walked

The miles I have walked have been many and far.

I grew up in Taiwan and Thailand as a daughter of a missionary. After college in the United States, I returned to Thailand. My friends were involved in providing human rights assistance to refugees and internally displaced persons from Burma.

Grim reality faced the people I encountered. Realities that are difficult to understand; rape, sex slavery, torture, humans used as landmine sweepers, child labor, unjust imprisonment, and the burning of rice fields.

The footsteps I would choose were inspired by the legacy of Aung San Suu Kyi fighting courageously for the democracy of her people. Democratically elected in 1990, a military regime threw out the votes and placed her under house arrest, but she continued to advocate for her people. Aung San Suu Kyi won the Nobel Peace Prize in 1991.

I have walked from Milwaukee, Wisconsin to Washington D.C.

While traveling in Costa Rica, a vision formed to walk. The walk would raise funds and awareness for Burmese refugees and internationally displaced persons. My brother, two friends, and I walked the complete journey. Although many joined up with us for support at various points. We walked to support those who had no choice but to walk, to run, for their lives.

A Walk for Burma:

- We walked 12 to 15 miles a day.

- We walked together and we walked apart in contemplation as the days stretched forward.

- Sandwiches and bread with condiments from fast food restaurants made up our meals.

- While we walked we carried all our clothes, food, and camping equipment. And at night we slept in tents in people's backyards.

- We spoke of the people of Burma at every yard we stayed and with every person who stopped along the way to ask about our journey.

- We walked east through sections of eight different states.

- One thousand miles total.

- 71 days.

- We walked as hope and in solidarity for the people of Burma.

At night we sought places to rest and sleep in people's yards, telling them why we walked. One family in Indiana opened their home to us by gathering friends and pulling together a cookout. That hospitality extended as they invited us to spend our rest day with them swimming in their pool, grilling and trying out a potato gun. They opened their home to us, and we felt the love of God through them. The next day when we reached our destination and returned to our campsite this same family jumped from the trees in surprise, bearing the gifts of hot pizza, cold drinks, and firewood. They became our temporary traveling family. These strangers we had only met days before.

Weariness followed us the last two weeks of walking. On day 71 we walked along a historic canal in Washington DC and right up to the White House. We ate a meal with members of an exiled Burmese community. A representative of Congress met with us and listened to our journey for the people of Burma.

The miles I have walked have been many and far.

I felt called to return to Thailand where I established Thai Village. A small work-study program emerged from the Bible Institute where my dad taught. The economy in the United States faltered and our funding struggled. We combined the natural handmade crafts skills of our students and their families with the emerging market of fair trade and cause-based consumers. Funding did not arrive and the institute closed, in response we began a self-supporting church through the income of the handicrafts program.

Local people have arrived the last two years desperately needing work. The people we see have not had the privilege of much education. They are single moms, former prisoners, and those stuck in poverty.

We see them. The people are bright, full of innate talents and skills, and open to learning more. We extend opportunities for them to generate income. They make beautiful handmade items.

As I walk alongside the people of Thailand, I have learned what helping means. What is important is not the giving, but the empowering. I witness people excel in their work, provide for their families, and plan for a secure future. The generosity of supporters humbles me. Whether a person is from a small village in Thailand, a big city in the west, a fair trade shop in Australia, or a University in Minnesota they all hold equal importance in the process.

It is only because we are a group of people working together that hope happens.
We make a difference when we walk these miles together, gathering strength from one another as we move forward.

Ghostwritten by: Lisa Van Engen

Author: Elizabeth Meinster

Born and raised in Asia, Elizabeth has lived in four countries, and traveled to over thirty. She loves experiencing the diversity of people around the world and the grandeur of nature. She is always seeking an adventure.

Thaivillage.org

Pain's Companion

"You like a sandwich, dear? 'Ave you eaten?" her northern accent drifted gently from the kitchen of the small London flat.

"No thank you, Ruth," I responded, taking my place on the couch of the cozy living room. The tangled disorder of leaves and blossoms printed on the antique sofa perfectly complemented the cluttered comfort of the entire flat. Heavily trinketed surfaces competed tirelessly with framed photographs in a fight to own the room.

"A cuppa tea then? You mus' be freezin', as chilly as it is." Ruth's persistent generosity won me over earlier each time I visited.

"That'd be great, thanks," I succumbed.

"I'll put the kettle on then." The kettle faintly gargled as Ruth wandered slowly into the room to join me. Each step was taken gingerly as breath struggled in and out of her lungs. She used her hand to brush down her thin white hair. After a short pause to find the chair behind her, she started a dramatically slow descent. This continued until about half a foot from the cushion of her recliner. Then, as though her muscles gave out all at once, she fell between the comfy arms of her favorite seat, letting out a painful groan.

Ruth looked at me grinning as she panted for air, "I've only been to the kitchen..." She let out a small giggle, took a breath and then continued, "...an' look at me. Can't even catch my breath." The end of her sentence trailed into a jolly laugh that floated into my gut and tickled me from the inside. I laughed along.

"Well," she took another deep breath, "how are you, Drew dear? Are you well?"

"Yeah, everything's going well," a half truth.

"You enjoying yourself at the church then?"

"Yeah, everything's great." I forced a smile, carrying on using my continuous evolving spiel about our youth work.

"That's good dear; you're doing a good work," she paused, looked around the room and apologized for an imaginary mess. I assured her it was alright, then she continued, "I am sorry I 'avn't made it to church. The Vicar must think me a terrible parishioner."

"It's alright Ruth, nobody minds. I am just glad I could stop by."

Our conversation continued to wander down its usual trail. We laughed, cursed the weather, forgot about the tea, and discuss things neither of us really cared about.

She had such a joy about her, rare in a woman of her age and situation, an eighty-something year old widow. Our visits always injected my heart with a warmth that slowly pumped its way through my cold limbs. She offered a comfort that I hungered for. A sense of family. Her tiny flat was a safe house, this couch a sanctuary from the frigid and stormy weather.

Once the pleasantries of small talk had run their course, Ruth would talk about her grandson in Canada, her only grandchild, and how much she missed him. She reckoned that my mother and grandmother in California must miss me "dreadfully". She'd ask me a question about them that she may have asked before, but I never minded reminding her of the answer. She would tell a story from the past, one that would make her laugh. And, as she occasionally did, she'd talk about John. This was a John visit.

Ruth's vision locked on something miles beyond the small wooden coffee table, as though she could see straight through it, and through the floor and deep into the earth. Eyes swelled, both hers and mine. "I miss him… so much," her lips trembled as the words shivered from her mouth. The words hung in the air like I a puff of smoke from a pipe. I could see them, smell them, feel them on the back of my teeth. Ruth wept.

In one way, I knew how she felt. I had built a room just like this. I spent my whole life filling it with comfort. A room built to forget real life. It was a retreat that I made my dwelling, a tiny cottage built in a hidden corner of my heart. The walls were constructed to hold the pain at bay, to shelter me from whatever might be menacing in the storm outside. But she was my constant companion, Pain. She was constricted around my chest and draped over my shoulders. I felt her weight always. I had given up hope to eradicate her. Instead my goal was to silence the continuous cries, to numb her touch. But I found that here, in this time, I could not escape her call; I had given up my frantic attempt to prop up these melting walls.

We sat in silence for a moment. Ruth changed the subject "…it's the arthritis you know."

"What do you mean?"

"The arthritis. It's what's keeping me from coming to church."

46

"My Dad has that. Says it's terrible. Keeps him up all night." I said

"Oh, it's so painful! I can hardly walk. I 'ave it in my hip so bad." She looked out the window, "but I cannot do it, Drew. I cannot sit in here all day.That's no way to live." It was as though she was speaking to me in my heart, challenging me to come out of my crumbling fortress. She continued, "sometimes things just hurt and that's life."

Ruth was right. God knew she was right, and he was prodding my soul with her words. Pain was not my enemy. In fact she was my ally, as God had intended her to be. Her wisdom pointed to neglected wounds that need attention, that need his healing. "Well, I'll let ya be on your way." And with that Ruth lifted herself weakly from her seat, and her strength lifted me from my couch, my comfort, my fear.

This story does not reflect a single interaction, but a collection of my true interactions and learnings with the woman known here as Ruth.

Author: Drew Tilton

Born: California 1987. Creative Writer, Blogger, Pastor. Helping others see God and turn to him.

DesertsWater.blogspot.com

Neon Sign

The buzz of the market was intoxicating, the bright colors dizzying, daring me to buy something exotic. Walking through a local market in the streets of Lima, Peru, fresh off of a trail woven through the Andes Mountains, I was feeling disoriented and overwhelmed. I was part of a group of 15 from my local church back home in suburban Atlanta Georgia. We had come with the mission of sharing the gospel to several remote villages tucked high in the Andes, armed with bibles written in the native Quechua language.

As a 22 year old fresh out of a relationship, taking a college hiatus, I was scrambling for any sort of direction and begging God for a neon sign pointing me towards my next path. I decided a path through the Andes was as good as any, and hoping I might have a life epiphany in the process, I had blindly put my name on the sign up sheet at church one Sunday. So here I was, standing in a Peruvian market, still searching for my neon sign.

My hand paused over an orange and pink scarf, not intending to buy anything, when I looked up into hungry eyes. She was a middle-aged woman, beaming with a ready smile that shone brightly out of her mocha skin and raven hair framed face. I noticed the vendor fanny pack secured around her waist, and felt a little uncomfortable with beginning my spill of "I'm just looking, I'm not planning on buying anything, thank-you-very-much".

"Why did you come here?" she asked in a boldly curious way.

"Excuse me?" I replied. What did she mean "here"? The market? Peru?

"Why did you come to my country?" she clarified in broken English.

In those brief seconds of contemplating what to say, I ran through my own personal reasons for coming to her country. To soul search myself, to get the heck out of dodge, for grand adventure, to match my brother's trans-global travels, for a silly crush, to try and forge friendships in a church where I wasn't quite connecting. Not exactly the answers to share. My mind darted to the proverbial Sunday school answer: Jesus!!! Yes, that was it, I came to tell people about Jesus.

"I came with my church from the United States to hand out Bibles in the mountains" I stumbled out.

"Do you have anymore?" she quickly, eagerly asked.

Do you mean I had just hiked for 5 days on treacherous trails, slept on the frozen ground, used a ditch for a bathroom, gotten lost in the dark atop a sheer mountain cliff, and this woman is going to straight up ASK for a bible? I don't have to go through the 5-point conversation starter to convince her she needs one? This is too easy! Except, we had no more bibles.

"I'm so, so sorry, I don't. We gave them all away" was my apologetic reply.

Her expression dropped and what flashed across her face was the real reason I'd come to Peru. Hunger for truth, a knowing that she couldn't be filled by anything better than the word of God, desperation to be seen and heard and loved. I saw my own soul written across her face. It's as if she was telling me what I was looking for when I boarded the plane 7 days ago in Atlanta.

"Can you read English?" I asked.

She nodded her head enthusiastically. "A little. Enough"

"I'll be right back". I ran faster than my trail weary legs wanted to go, weaving in and out of booths and the crowded streets, searching for our van that was scheduled to depart in less than 15 minutes. I flung open the doors and started searching for my red duffle bag. The bottom, of course, it was on the bottom. I clawed my way through to it, grasping for each grain of truth, jewel of wisdom, bread crumb of life that was contained inside. I was able to wiggle my hand in and feel for the leather bound pages and pull it out. I quickly stuffed everything I'd unearthed back into the van and slammed the doors shut, turned and made my way back to her.

Breathless, I shoved it into her hands. "Here. Take mine. Take my Bible. I want you to have it."
She reached out to take it, her eyes wide and swimming with emotion, as if she already understood the promises it contained for her.

Before I released it, I wrote my name, email, and mailing address in the front cover. She scribbled her name and contact information on a scrap of paper. Samanda. We would go on to email and write letters over the next year. I still have the rosary that she sent me that had been hers as a young girl.

I gave Samanda my bible on the streets of Lima. And she gave me a glimpse into my own desperate need. Not a need for world travel, high mountain adventure, or a soul-searching journey, but a need to return home to the truth and find my identity written on the pages of that leather bound book.

Author: Stephanie Hoffer

Stephanie is dirt-digging, PB&J-making, heart-shaping Mama of two darlings. Wife to a man of rock-solid character, she prays to live life with supernatural eyes, spotting God stories daily.

Lifetime Lessons

I remember it like yesterday. I was at home sick when I heard the front door open. My husband came into our bedroom with a look I'll never forget. He was as white as a sheet and looked dazed. I asked why he was home early and he said we needed to call my parents. Fear instantly overcame me.

As the phone began to ring my mind raced with the possibility of what I was going to hear. The heartache had already set in when my mom and dad answered the phone to my tearful, "what's going on?"

The next 30 minutes were a blur. Something about cancer, stage four, not curable, the Mayo Clinic, looking into options. I could barely catch my breath as the tears flowed down my cheeks. I remember barely being able to hold the phone, wishing I could hang up so that I didn't have to hear any more news, wishing I could rewind time to only minutes before when life was so much easier. When life didn't include my dad having cancer.

In that moment my family was standing at the edge of everyone's worst fear. What we couldn't imagine was also standing at the edge of our greatest lesson.

From a very early age, I watched my dad. I was a daddy's girl so I paid attention and learned all that I could to know him better, to be more like him.

I watched as he establish and nurtured relationships that felt more like family than friends. He poured time into many lives, but three men in particular. They were his friends, his brothers. They had a relationship that knew no bounds. These are the relationships that I grew up knowing, observing, and praying for.

I watched my dad give freely, generous with both his time and money. I remember him gifting cars, tools, computers, anonymous envelopes of cash, handy-man skills, and more. It was after my dad died that I learned of a generous act he bestowed on a single mom that worked for him. He offered to fill up her car with gas before she left on a road-trip with her two young kids. Little did she know, he not only filled up the car, he replaced all four worn down tires to make sure her family would be safe on the road. This was not uncommon. He was a generous man that taught me how important it is to give. My husband would tell you this was the greatest lesson he learned from my dad.

I watched my dad invest in the Wichita community, pouring into World Impact, The Urban Ministry Institute (TUMI) and young patients that sat in his orthodontic chair.

I watched my dad invest in our family. He founded a Christian high school with two other men in order to give me and my brother a Christian education. He founded a Christian Boy Scout troop in order to grow my brother and his friends into men with rock solid godly values. He was Grey Wolf at our Indian Princess meetings, investing in daddy/daughter dates with me. He was a baseball coach, a basketball coach, and a volleyball coach. He understood the importance of catching up around the dinner table, and the power of a family vacation. My dad poured his life into our family, and for that I will be a better parent and wife.

There are so many things I learned from watching my dad live his life. But the greatest lesson didn't take 28 years of observation. No, it only took two and it started the day I thought my world fell apart.

I watched my dad suffer through rounds of chemo, radiation, and the side effects that accompanied the two. A man that was often called the "energizer bunny" became fatigued and worn down. He had always been physically strong but he soon became undeniably aware of his limitations. His body ached from crippling headaches. His appetite went away, and when he did eat, most foods lost their taste. It was a new normal that no one should have to endure.

But it was there, in the valley, that my dad found a different *kind* of strength. He had a deep peace knowing that he was a child of God, knowing that heaven was near and the Lord was waiting his arrival. He took every opportunity to share his faith, even leading his 80 year-old mother to Christ after she asked why he had such great peace in the face of this nightmare. He never questioned his cancer, never asked, "why me?"

The greatest lesson I learned from my dad came a few weeks before he went home to the Lord. I remember sitting on his bed, watching him struggle through the miserable torment that medication no longer seemed to fully help. He told me that if all this was to happen again, he wouldn't change a thing. He wouldn't wish away the cancer. it had brought so many wonderful things, mainly his mother's salvation. He wouldn't choose to tear apart the tapestry the Lord was weaving around his life. He had complete faith that he served a big God who doesn't make mistakes. God uses the strong and capable, as well as the meak and mild, and because of that, my dad felt honored to be on the journey he was traveling.

I always say we have the great blessing of missing my dad. It's a blessing because not everyone gets to know a man as kind, loving, inspiring and generous as him. It's because he was such an amazing father, husband and friend that we miss him at all.

So we are blessed.

Blessed to have known him. To have learned from him. To have watched him live life. We look forward to the blessing of one day rejoining him.

In memory of Robert Smith, a true couch rebel.

Author: Abby Andrus

Wife. Sister. Daughter. Aunt. Friend. All titles I'm glad to own! Livin' life with my best friend/hubby while hunting adventures. Love the outdoors, cooking, travel and time with family and friends!

AdamandAbbysAdventures.blogspot.com

What Color is 'Sad'?

"What color is 'happy'?"

The compassionate therapist was teaching me and my 8 year old adopted son about discussing our feelings in colors, rather than in words.

Children (and adults) recovering from trauma can't easily associate words with their pain. To give the past words would be to give it even more power. So, silence protects the past, locking it in a formless safe-house.

She repeated the question to little Dalton, my 5th child.
He whispered, "Blue."
"What about 'angry'?"
"Between dark green and light green."

He doesn't look up. His focus is on making the popping noise in the putty his hands wrap around, rather than focus on the dreaded popping sounds of his first three years of life.

"What about 'sad'?"
"Ummmmm, clear. "
"So, sad is clear?"
"Yep."

Clear.
Empty.
Vacant.
Like air.

It's there. Surrounding him, filling his lungs, but he can't see it. If it's clear, it doesn't affect him in any way – and all the while, the air controls every oxygenated beat of his bleeding heart.

See through.
Transparent.
Avoidance of what is. The dodging of reality so he can live in color.
Dark.
Red.
Shadows.
Fire.

His nose was broken at just three years old. Hours after this ER trip, he and his twin sister were removed from the only home they had ever known, and placed in foster care.

Brain trauma runs deep. The fiery red zone that several therapists speak of - is the rush of adrenaline – a fight or flight instinct, used to protect and defend the victim from the one throwing punches.

Dalton lived here – in survival mode - from birth to age three –the most formative years. What is formed here is the norm for all the years ahead.

So his options were 1.) Red hot, rushing heat, fear gripping his heart, or 2.) Go transparent, turned off, all alone, walled in.

He erased.
He forgot.
He pretended.

He has a gift for hiding. How could he not?
He was the twin un-chosen.
The twin that didn't win his mother's heart, but rather, the one
who watched his sister be held, loved, kept.

They say Reactive Attachment Disorder is common in abused
children, and there are varying levels to the shut down and
distance a child keeps so close.

R.A.D.
Radically-Altogether-Distant.
Really-Adamantly-Defensive.

Dalton lives far away from me yet close enough to touch. He's
been officially mine for a few years now, and yet, feels like a
complete stranger sometimes.

How could a boy want to know another mom when his first one
allowed such damage? When her heart neglected, deflected,
and caused his to be defective.

A good friend of mine, who has worked through years of
childhood sexual abuse, explained to me what the fiery red zone
feels like to her. She's in her fifties, and the abuse comes alive in
mere fractions of a second, even though she's done years of
forgiveness – intentional healing work - even with hope breaking
the pain – it still surfaces, just as fiercely.

Recently, while heading home from a mountain trip, she lunched
in her hometown, at her teenage hangout, with her young adult
daughter. Lunch was light, remembering was fun.

And then it fired. Burning of her shadowed memories- floodgates of rage surfaced above her head, trapping her heart – just like he had – her damaging parent, perpetrator of her tender innocence.

She said to me, after this intense recall: "It came back as if it was happening all over again. Every time he came in my room, was wrapped into that one moment. Every lie spoken, every empty word thrown, consumed me – in one deep breath."

Fire.
Burns.
Fierce.
Fast.
And furious.

One second - the red zone rages from brain to body, from head to heart, from top to bottom and sends her right back to defense - to survival of the fittest.

And she's in her fifties. She's had years to heal.
He's just a little boy.

Only five years removed from the night in the ER, when his mom screamed at doctors and police officers – "No one f***in' hit him!"
"Leave me the f***alone!"
"Take him if you want. Take her too, for all I care."

I read the words she had spoken that night - after the adoption was final.
They handed the twins their teddy bears in court that day, and placed in my hands, piles of evidence, years of pain, safely tied up in four green folders.

Green folders full of red and white and black and blue.

Ripe with abuse and neglect, the choosing of men over children.

The mother that did her best to raise them, she'd been wrecked with pain and neglect too.

What else would she have handed down to them? All she knew was becoming a mom at age 13, losing that child to a visit with her father, then a few years later, giving birth to twins.

Their father would beat her so bloody she crossed state lines just to stay alive.

Blood-red memories.

A black and blue trail of suffering.

Can all be made clear, in one thought, one spark - one fire? Shutdown mode can be immediate - sadness won't be allowed to take over the mind of the broken.

Just like his birth mom, he does the best he can to connect. His shallow hugs, his shell of a body against mine - I try to find a piece of him. I reach. And miss.

One day, his sad and clear will become colorful and bright, and he will share about his pain. He won't have to hide behind his protective walls, all alone.

If I could take the past away, I would.
If I could convince his heart that I am not her, that I'm me, I would reassure him.

Let me in, Buddy. I'm doing my best to color you with love.

"What color is 'confused'?" She asked quietly.
45 seconds. 30 beats of his heart.
He couldn't answer. Not yet.

Author: Jenny Price

Pastor's wife. I like my husband. Mom of five. I love teenagers. My twins mold my heart. Blogger. Coach. Mentor. Friend. I bleed hope. I hold onto what I profess in Christ - and I want to help you do the same.

iwokeupyesterday.com

Obedience and Adventure

The call to Ethiopia was surprisingly simple.

My husband and I saw the announcement in the church bulletin and felt, almost immediately, we would like to go-despite us leaving our one-, three-, and five-year-old at home for over two weeks, my husband leaving work, and the fact that we had never considered going on any kind of mission trip ever before. God called us to go, and gave us incredible peace about the decision. He cleared our path, at each step of the trip, and we strove to follow Him, although we weren't yet sure why He called us to there.

When my husband and I decided we needed to say 'yes' to this trip, my prayer above all things, was that I would just give it my all. I wanted to be Jesus' hands and feet; I wanted to love others with an open heart like His; I wanted my insecurities and any fears to not get in the way. I wanted my heart to be open to be fully used by God. I didn't want to come home with any regrets.

I had no idea that the turning point for me, of all our trip's amazing experiences, would be the moments I spent on the side of a road, with a blind boy asking for change.

When I was exiting a tour of a church, in Lalibella, a young blind boy began following me, his right hand outstretched, saying over and over, "I am blind, one birr?"

I was so uncomfortable. I didn't know what to do. At another time in my life, before this trip, I may have walked faster, or given him money. I don't know. But I do know I wouldn't have even thought about trying to get to know a little blind beggar, or have a conversation. I would not have touched him; I would not have introduced myself and taken his hand. When walking from the church, though, with him still following, my heart began to break for this little boy, and I began to think about what I could do.

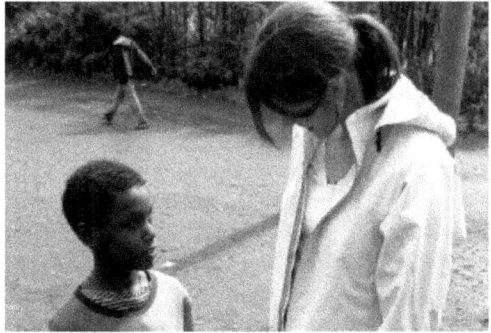

I thought about what Jesus would do, and how He might heal him. I knew I couldn't do that, and I was so frustrated. I also knew I couldn't give this child any money; our group leaders had told us it was unwise to do so. So, I had to think about what I could do - and I just knew I had to love this child. Finally, I turned to the boy, took his hand, and asked him his name. He didn't seem to hear me at first, and kept repeating his plea for one birr.

I told him I couldn't give him any money, but I asked his name. "My name is Jennifer." I touched his shoulder, leaned toward him, and told him that Jesus loves him... Jesus loves him...

I still didn't think I was getting through. But when I asked him how old he was, something changed, and he heard me.

He seemed a little surprised with the question, and then he answered, "I am ten years old." I told him that he is so tall for ten years old, and he seemed so proud . . . and the most amazing thing happened . . . he smiled. I told him how big and strong he is going to be when he grew up. Again he beamed. I asked him what his favorite game was, and if he liked to play football.

"Yes, futball", he replied with a huge smile.

This little blind beggar boy with flies near his mouth, a small wooden cane in his left hand... smiled.

My heart had broken for this little boy, and God had told my heart what to do. I am thankful for the Father, my Teacher, showing me during that trip, how to love better. I need to seek Him and follow, so I can more authentically love others.

My trip to Ethiopia gave me new eyes to see, and a new passion for people. It taught me a new way to love. More than anything, it showed me how to be fully present with someone, and give them everything I have, in that moment, so I can better see them. And, sometimes, my heart broke, but mostly, I was filled with God's peace and His joy.

One of my biggest struggles now, being back home, is seeing God in the same way I saw Him in Ethiopia. Again, I struggle with slowing down, with striving to be a vessel for God to pour out His love for his children. But now I see the possibilities, and the hope, and how my heart is different when I walk with Him and I follow the path He clears for me-rather than trying to clear my own. There is such a difference between me trying to chop through the forest rather than trusting God to clear my path for me, and then strive to walk in His footsteps. It's not for me to say that God's path is going to be the easier path, but it will be the path that He helps me navigate, and shows me how to soar through.

Author: Jennifer Camp

Voice finder; wife of a heart-warrior; mom of three; encourager of My Girls; God seeker; outdoor lover; womens' heart pursuer; my desire is to live in my true identity, in God's eyes.

YouAreMyGirls.com

Life Was Good and All Was Well...

My wife and I are both sitting in Cambodia right now — a place we never in a million years thought we'd be. We were quite content in our cozy, comfortable home, and we felt we did our part: I played guitar and sang in the church band, my wife helped with church functions. We were both nice to those around us, and we loved our family and friends. Life was good, and all was well.

That changed, though, when the Daraja Children's Choir of Africa came to our town to do a concert raising awareness for needy children in developing countries. This concert was at our church, and our Worship Band was going to perform alongside them.

The night of practice, I sat in the parking lot, waiting for the Daraja troupe to finish their main rehearsal. All was quiet, then a rush of Kenyan kids and host families burst out of the doors. Everyone was running, skipping, playing — just having a blast. I should have been happy like everyone else, but I found myself getting irritated. Not being a "kid person," I felt completely inadequate not being able to connect with those kids the way I was seeing everyone else connect. I was jealous — jealous of our friends who were living outside of themselves, stepping out of their comfort zones.

Along comes Sunday, and I'm on stage playing the songs the kids are performing to. As great as this was, it was tainted with the inadequacy I still felt — but something was about to happen. During one of the songs, the group leader looked over at me, gave a nod, and beamed me this huge smile. When he did that, something inside me broke. Tears just began pouring, and I was barely able to keep it together. God had grabbed my heart and course-changed my life forever in that instant, and that was the beginning of my life as I know it now.

I was no longer content sitting on my sofa, watching TV night after night. I could no longer just build guitar effects pedals for a living. I could no longer just hang out with family and friends. It just wasn't enough anymore, and I had to do something.

My Pastor has always encouraged our church members to go on at least one foreign mission trip before we die, and he has a tremendous love for Cambodia. Before Daraja, I never wanted to step foot outside the USA unless it was to go on a posh vacation — but things had changed. With his encouragement, and the encouragement of those around us, we decided to make a trip to Cambodia and see the country he (and so many others from our church) loved so much.

We fell in love the moment our feet hit the ground.

Cambodia was the Life Change God put into our hearts, and from this, our non-profit, Threaded Leaf Project was born. We now wake up and spend each day working to thread hope toward brighter futures for women, children, and students in Cambodia.

If we would have stayed on the couch, we wouldn't have the relationship we have with Jariya, one of our clothing accessory crocheters. She's an acid attack survivor, and she's shunned by society and her peers because of her appearance. We're able to give her — and other acid attack survivors — consistent employment when no one else will. In the years we've worked with these survivors, we've become shoulders to cry on, friends to laugh with, and our lives are better for knowing them all.

If we would have stayed on the couch, we wouldn't have the relationship we have with Bopha, our clothing line's Head Seamstress. She's not only accomplished with needle and thread, she has a heart with a desire to help those less fortunate. As she assembled a team of seamstresses for us, she sought out women in desperate need of consistent employment. These ladies are now able to provide for their families even when their husbands are struggling to find work. They used to work alone all day at their homes, but they now work alongside Bopha, laughing together, sharing together, growing closer. It's wonderful to see these women growing in self-worth, value, and in community. The ladies told Bopha they don't sew for money anymore — they sew for love. We're honored to call all these women our friends.

If we would have stayed on the couch, the old Maury and Karen wouldn't have the relationship we have with our students — a group of seven amazing kids that we love as though they were our own. Some of them are orphans, some are from the countryside, and some still have family in the city. Through our scholarship program, they all have hope for a brighter future through education — something they never thought possible. The best part is that the guy that wasn't a "kid person" can't think of anything he'd rather be doing than spending time with all of them, and we're blessed to be able to do just that. We're here investing in each of their lives, loving them, encouraging them face-to-face. You just can't beat it.

I could spend hours telling story after story about the people we get to work with, but the bottom line is this: our lives wouldn't be where they are if we hadn't been willing to get off the couch. We had every reason to continue living our easy life, so why risk it? Why leave it all behind? Because you never know what amazing things are out there waiting for you. You never know who you may meet, and how your life might be forever changed.

Get off the couch and find YOUR journey. For me, it started with a Kenyan choir which led us to Cambodia. For you, it may be at home, work, or school. It's out there somewhere — and it's SO worth finding.

Author: Maury McCown

My heart and soul are in Cambodia, and, together with my wife, we operate Threaded Leaf Project - a non-profit working to improve the lives of students, women, and children in Cambodia.

ThreadedLeafProject.org

The Route Revision

One idea and one obstacle changed my life. Forever.

The idea was mine: "Let's start from Jiri."

Jiri is a small village in Nepal, a 7-8 day hike from the Lukla airport, the starting point for most trekkers bound for Everest Base Camp. Jiri to Lukla is a week of hard straight up and straight down hiking, but amazingly beautiful and not the crowded circus encountered after the airport. I penciled out an itinerary that came up with a 24-day trek, turned to my (now ex-) wife, and said, "Let's start from Jiri."

The obstacle was hers: "I am not hauling a backpack for 24-days."

I knew by the definitive way she spoke it was no use, but I tried: "But you only need to pack a toothbrush, one change of clothes, a sleeping bag, . . ." "I am not hauling a backpack for 24-days." To overcome this obstacle we hired a porter from a trekking agency.

I was expecting a grizzled Sherpa with coffee-can calves and altitude-hardened skin. We got Tanka: a small, 22-year old, clean-cut university student earning his tuition hauling tourists' overstuffed bags up the mountain. "Really? This little guy?"

Tanka was more than up to the task, and even brought along his textbooks so he could study since he was missing classes for the trek. I think his textbooks weighed more than our stuff.

For 24 days we traveled together. You get to know someone pretty well when you travel with them, and on days you quickly gain the maximum 300 meters in altitude, there's a lot of acclimatization time to talk, solve the world's problems, and ponder the quirks of the English language ("I don't know why 'telephone' is not spelled with an 'F'"). Over 24 days, Tanka and I connected.

The trek to Everest Base Camp was magical and life-enriching, but that's not what this story is about. This story starts a year later in September 2001. I had just taken a contract job in New York City when Tanka emailed, "I am working a trek with two Americans who are hiking up from Jiri leaving on the same day you did with almost the same route. Funny, huh?"

No. Not funny. Here was this intelligent, resourceful, determined young man squandering away his university time as a mule. I told him as much. I already knew that his tuition, books, room & board were about US $100 a month – pocket change in New York City. I made him an offer: cancel this trip, agree to never haul another bag, and I would sponsor his last 2.5 years of university.

He said "No." He didn't want to be in debt, and have to pay me back. I clarified, "You don't pay me back, you pay it forward. When you're older and established, do something big for someone else." He agreed.

Fast-forward four years. Now a university graduate, Tanka had his "pay-it-forward" idea: he wanted to build a primary school in his village. He was the only one of seven siblings allowed to make the long hike to the nearest school. On our Everest trek, Tanka and I often discussed that education is the key to a better Nepal, a better world. "We will build it," he said, "but we need money for materials. Can you help?"

71

The budget was millions of Nepali Rupees but translated to only about US $14,000. I did my homework and found that yeah, in Nepal you can build a 7-room school for $14,000. I sent a letter to everyone I knew asking them, "Instead of spending money on a night out this weekend, will you send me a check?" They did. Tanka built his school: The Devisthan Primary School in Khari, Nepal opened in January 2006 with 125 smiling K-5 students.

I first returned to Nepal in 2007 and was amazed at the impact this little school was having on not only the children but the whole community. I also learned something important: little kids grow up! What were the Grade 6 kids going to do? Tanka and I decided that they would go to school.

Partnering with the community, The Baladevi School was built and opened in January 2009. Intended as a secondary school, so many parents brought their K-5 students – who had no other school to attend – that the local School Management Committee decided they could not turn them away and quickly revised the plan. Today, Baladevi is a K-10 school with 351 students, most of whom would otherwise have no access to education.

You want *life changing*? Go live in a rural Nepali village for a month as I did in September 2010 and jump completely off the grid. No electricity, no running water. Eat what you grow, no contact outside the village, and certainly no internet. It's like stepping back in time 300 years. It was challenging, insightful, and rewarding - a time full of thought and self-discovery.

Six days a week I taught English to children who previously had no school to attend, and their enthusiasm to learn astounded me. The children grasped what an education could do for them. Fourth graders often had more knowledge in the basics of mathematics, social studies, grammar – and certainly English – than their parents. And those parents beamed with pride.

These schools were changing lives in a powerful way, and I discovered within myself a passion to keep it going. Thus, I founded The Global Community For Education and made this grassroots effort "official." With support from both loyal and new donors, we're continuing to help make this world just a little bit better place – one school at a time.

GCE's slogan is "Building Schools. Changing Lives." I find it ironic that the slogan is directed at the children, yet my life has been immensely enhanced by my experiences. So keep your eyes, mind, and heart open: one simple idea or one unexpected obstacle may forever change your life.

Author: Don Wilks

Don's life is guided by two beliefs: travel provides life's greatest education, and leave this world better than you found it. He has created a "Voluntarily Unemployed" life to pursue these beliefs.

GlobalCommunityForEducation.org

Providing Comfort

The convenience store was busy that Friday evening. Nestled in the middle of the desert, 50 miles from the nearest town, travelers pulled off the freeway for their last chance of gas, snacks or a bathroom break. Every parking stall was taken in the crowded lot, until one opened up right in front.

As I sat in my car with my two dogs waiting for my daughter to return with snacks I saw him. Sitting on a bench was an apparent homeless man. He quietly took in the activity around him with a faraway look. Dirty and lonely he watched numerous people pass.

Nobody seemed to notice. They walked by as if he were a statue. And I thought *why*?

Do they not want to notice? Do they not care? Do they not want to get involved? Do they cast blame? Do they really even see him?

My daughter returned and I got out for my break. I entered the store contemplating those questions. I thought to myself, who am I kidding? I am they. I don't want to notice or care either. How did he get there and why doesn't he just get a job!

As I left the store I walked up to him. Unsure of the outcome, I placed my hand on his bony shoulder. I had read somewhere that homeless people seldom feel a loving touch. I asked him if he needed anything, I would get him some food or water if he wanted.

He looked up and grinned, surprised someone stopped. His countenance seemed to change before my very eyes. He said, "Well... I need some cigarettes."

An internal argument ensued in my mind. I wasn't prepared for his answer. I was ready to buy food or water, but not cigarettes. I had asked him what he needed and he answered truthfully. If that was his need, then why not?

I told him that I would get some money out of my car and he followed me the short distance. Knowing I would not have done this if I were alone, I was secure knowing my daughter and two large dogs were there for security.

I asked my daughter to hand me $5.00; I knew that's all I had. As she handed it to me I thought it may not be enough. I asked how much cigarettes were and he replied $5.40. My daughter and I scrounged for loose change as he waited patiently on the curb.

I returned and handed him the money. He appreciatively held out his hand to thank me. As I held out mine, I instantly felt compelled to hug him, once again called off the couch and out of my comfort zone.

I stepped up on the curb and spread my arms. He wrapped *his* arms around me and squeezed. His bony frame felt frail and he smelled from sitting in the desert heat without showering, but I didn't care. He was a human being, in need of feeling loved. He clung to me like his life depended on it.

As we separated, he said to me sheepishly, "I have been down and out for 2½ years. It has been hard, and at times I just wanted a touch from someone, but people are so standoffish. Wanting a hug is asking the impossible. But I asked God, as I prayed last night, for a hug today! Thank you!"

I returned to my car, and when I closed the door the tears began, flowing so uncontrollably I was unable to tell my daughter what had just transpired. I was full of emotion, and grateful I'd listened to that small inner voice from the Holy Spirit, I sobbed.

My daughter thought he'd said something mean and had hurt my feelings, but when I was able to tell her, she also cried.

Six months later I returned to that popular stop and there he sat. I walked up to him and reminded him of being there months prior and that I'd given him a hug, then asked if he remembered me. With a look of joy that was indescribable he stood up and answered, "Yes! Yes I remember you!"

It was the beginning of a friendship between us. My husband and I stop by to see Jerry frequently. We take him money, clothes, food or whatever he may need. We have also shared about Jerry with our friends, now others are also stopping by and helping him out.

Sometimes we are called to get off our couch to provide comfort to someone else.

Author: Dana Rausch

I've been married 33 years, have three adult children and four granddaughters. I am currently working on a book on marriage. I love to blog and share life experiences through picture stories.

ApplyYourHeart.com

Darkness to Light: A Story of Redemption and Life

My life changed forever at the age of 19 when I had an unplanned pregnancy. Growing up in a pro-life family I never dreamed my beliefs would be tested. It was much less complicated to think of it as a pregnancy, rather than as a baby.

I knew what I had to do: have an abortion.

Face the consequences of my actions; tell my family what I had done; shame them with an unplanned, teenage pregnancy before marriage; carry and deliver a baby; have shattered plans for my future; or possibly go through the pain that is sure to come with adoption? No, I simply couldn't. I was weak and vulnerable. I had no other choice, or so I thought. If I had known the depression and guilt that would follow, I would have chosen a different path. But, in the midst of my heartache and despair, I regret having to say that's not the choice I made. I convinced myself that ending my pregnancy at only six weeks' gestation wasn't really an abortion. I wish I had known that my child's tiny heart had already begun beating.

Having an abortion has to be okay because it's legal, I thought to myself. The culture I lived in told me it was my choice and that it wasn't a big deal. How did I start to believe the lies? My spirit was breaking over this decision, this impending loss. The tears were proof of this. The tears were proof that deep inside, my heart knew that I was already a mother who was carrying her first babe.

On February 6, 2009, I took the RU-486 pill, and after a night of darkness, it was over. I was relieved to get back to my normal life. I wanted to move on as if the nightmare never happened, and forget the immense pain. I was deceived into thinking that I could forget about it. The counselor at Planned Parenthood had told me that some initial sadness after my abortion would be normal, but after a couple days, if I was still feeling depressed, that wouldn't be normal, and I should seek help. How wrong she was. Much of those days before and after my abortion are a blur of heartbreak and tears. Sleepless nights were spent with agony at the depths of my heart and soul, rattling me to the core. There was nothing "wrong" with me for feeling that way.

Trying to forget what I had done, over the next few months, I sought comfort for my wounded, aching heart through partying, drinking, and living promiscuously. I was digging myself deeper and deeper into a pit of destruction and despair.

Four months after my abortion, I was pregnant...again.

I fooled myself into thinking I would get my life together after what I thought was another necessary abortion. The appointment was set at Planned Parenthood...

However, Jesus was fighting for me and for my unborn baby. God showed me that if I chose to have another abortion, I couldn't imagine the pain and darkness that would follow. But if I chose *life*, I couldn't imagine the real beauty that He would bring...

Instead of walking through those clinic doors a second time, I chose to walk into the light towards freedom. It was as if the reasoning for abortion fell away when I knew that God would be with me every step of my difficult journey. I was at peace knowing I was making the right choice – the choice of life...

On March 16, 2010, ready to deliver my full-term daughter, I was told the devastating news that her perfect little heart was no longer beating. I had to deliver the body of my precious flower, Lily Katherine, who had already whispered goodbye before I said hello. I had to give her enough hugs and kisses to last a lifetime. I watched as her tiny white casket was lowered into the opened earth and was showered with tears, rose and lily petals, and dirt.

My entire life and future has been changed by two babies who never spoke a word or took a breath. Yet God is speaking through them, saying just how precious and valuable each individual life is. He has a plan and purpose for each beautiful life created in His image. He can take our deepest sorrow and sin and work them together for our good and His glory! Through choosing life for my second child, God brought peace and healing to my heart that was broken from aborting my first.

Luke Shiloh and Lily Katherine, I once wanted to be rid of you and hoped nobody would ever find out you even existed. Now, I want the world to know you are my children. I promise to always be your voice and to honor you in whatever way I can for as long as I live.

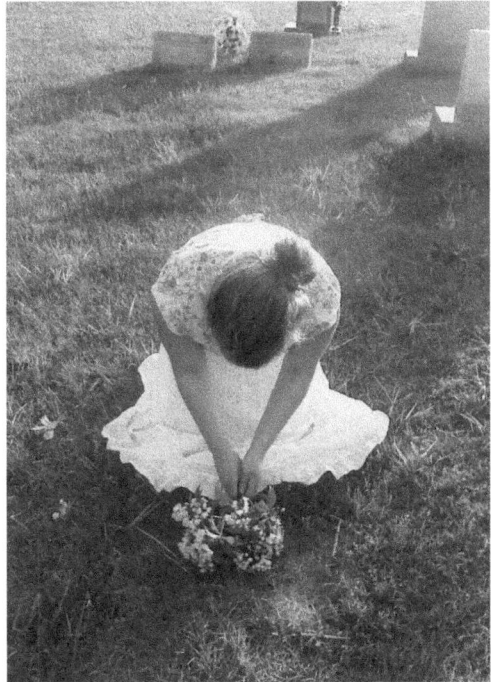

Sharing my story isn't easy. Yet it's because of this promise to my two children of Heaven and my desire to bring glory to

Jesus Christ that I do share. Because of the lives of my two little ones, I have a passion and a purpose that I wouldn't have if I hadn't had these experiences. I now share my story, both on my own blog, as well as on other websites, and hope to write a book one day soon. I also travel the country, sharing my story at banquets, pro-life events, churches, college campuses, conferences, rallies, and so forth. I volunteer at my local Pregnancy Resource Center and plan on getting involved in post-abortive ministry. I want to inspire others to get involved in pro-life ministry. Never feel like you are just one life and cannot make a difference... look at how two children who never took a single breath have changed my life completely, forever! As an introvert, speaking out publicly on one of the most controversial topics today is definitely out of my comfort zone!

Author: Hannah Rose Allen

Through her own experience with unplanned pregnancy, abortion and the loss of a child, Hannah Rose has become dedicated to ministering the love of Jesus to others, as a writer and speaker.

Roseandherlily.com

Raising a Couch Rebel

I am a mom.

I have never traveled the world. I have never saved an endangered species or been to a third world country. I have never helped fund missions or taken a spontaneous trip with nothing more than the money in my pocket.

I have however followed my dreams. And I am most certainly raising my daughter to do the same.

To an outsider, my life must seem average or mundane.

To me, my life is adventurous; each day more beautiful than the last. Each day a new opportunity to do something great, learn something new, enjoy my family.

I have learned over the years that we don't have to do extraordinary things to be extraordinary people. We are all called to lead lives of different magnitudes. We follow different paths, but we all have a purpose.

At eighteen years old I married my highschool sweetheart. People thought we were out of our minds. "They will realize the mistake they made." They would say.

That was five years ago.

I have never been one to take advice, even when the advice being given is wise and well meaning (sorry mom.) If I am told "you can't," I will. If I am told "you shouldn't" I am even more certain that I should.

I follow my heart more than my head. I follow my dreams whether practical or not. Marrying at eighteen was interesting to say the least but it was the start of an amazing journey that continues to get better every day.

My husband and I had been married for only a few short months when we found out that I have endometriosis. This disease can be very damaging to a woman's fertility. My doctor said that my chances of conceiving naturally were not all that great. To me that sounded a lot like "you can't." And we all know what I say to that.

I was scared. I wanted children. I wanted to raise a family.

I met endometriosis head on. I underwent surgery and an intense treatment of induced menopause. My body felt like it had been hijacked for well over a year. I hardly recognized the person I saw in the mirror. Some days I would sit and wonder if all of the trouble was truly worth it. What if I went through all of this and I still could not conceive a child?

Fortunately the treatment paid off. Two years after undergoing treatment we found out we were expecting a baby!

The flood of emotions I experienced in those first few moments was overwhelming. I was excited, nervous, scared, happy, and confused. I was going to be a mom. At the time I was working in a law firm. I had been there for several years and earned a comfortable paycheck. I had never given any serious thought to what I would do with regards to work and childcare. It had always been a topic that I felt would be addressed when the time came.

Well the time was here and decisions needed to be made. As my pregnancy progressed I began to feel a tug deep within my heart. With every sonogram I began to fall more deeply in love with the tiny fingers, toes, and facial features of my precious baby to be. Every time I heard the precious sound of her heartbeat, I was even more sure that it was the most beautiful sound I had ever heard in my entire life.

I found myself focusing more and more on preparing for motherhood and less and less on the stacks of files and endless phone calls I would receive on my desk each day.

At six months pregnant I was put on bed rest due to complications. This afforded me not only the rest that my baby and I needed, but also endless time to bond with my unborn child. I read to her, I sang to her, I talked to her. Slowly she became my life.

Although I had not made a final decision, I knew in my heart that once this sweet baby was born, I would never be able to tear myself away.

On the day of our daughter's birth, a part of me became alive that I never knew was dormant. As I cradled this sweet new life in my arms and looked into the eyes of my newborn child I knew that I was born to be a mom.

I never went back to work.

It was scary...

My husband and I had to do some financial adjusting and we learned to live as a single income family. Any sacrifices that we have had to make have been well worth it. Nothing brings us greater pleasure than to see our daughter happy and thriving.

I may not have traveled the world. I may not be living a life of adventure and spontaneity. But I am living a life filled with love and purpose, and I am raising my child to know that she can reach beyond the stars to achieve her wildest dreams. I am raising a couch rebel. My daughter will not know the meaning of the words "I can't" but will instead know the meaning of the words "I will."

I stepped outside of my comfort zone into the world of motherhood. A precious life had been placed in my hands; a life that I am now responsible for molding, shaping, and encouraging.

I am a mother and I am raising my child to know that there are no boundaries when it comes to achieving her goals. Every day I witness my daughter reach new milestones, master new skills, and discover the world around her. I cannot wait to see what her future holds. Whether she becomes a seasoned world traveler, a doctor, an artist, or a mom…. I am going to be right there cheering her on and watching her grow into the beautiful woman she is destined to become.

Author: Jillian Amodio

Jillian is an author, writer, wife, and mother. There is no job she finds more rewarding than being a mom. Jillian writes on a variety of topics mostly pertaining to family and parenting.

JillianAmodio.com

Covered in Honey and Left for Dead

I grew up in a very affluent, comfortable, sheltered environment right in the middle of the Bible-belt. My worldview was narrow and my concern for issues outside of myself were limited. Some of this was due to the fact that I was a recent high school graduate more concerned with how I was going to decorate my upcoming dorm room and how I was going to get through a recent break-up rather than the social injustices that I could not see. However, things began to change when I took my first trip to India.

I ventured to a western region of India with my family the summer after I graduated high school. My eyes were opened to the realities of sex-trafficking, hopelessness, poverty, disease, filth, greed, corruption, and abuse. The people were beautiful, times of worship with believing Christians was powerful, and the colors and textures were something to behold. The most stunning thing however, was the contrast between the beauty and the bleak, wealth and poverty, joy and pain. After one trip I was hooked and knew I needed to go back. My worldview was changing and my eyes had been opened.

The opportunity came about for me to do an internship in India for my college degree. I chose to team up with a family who helped run a school for underprivileged children as well as a home that had taken in girls who were rescued from female infanticide. At the time this didn't mean much more to me other than an exciting adventure and a chance to complete the requirements of my degree. I quickly realized that it was going to be far more than just that.

We walked into the "girls home" and were instantly surrounded by twenty-two precious little girls, all under the age of five. They were eager for our attention and affection and as we gave them each a hug their little faces beamed with delight. They asked us to sing with them and we began to sing, "Making melodies in my heart to the King of Kings; Thumbs Up!, Elbows Out!, Knees Bent!" We watched them delightedly follow our lead and join along, each one melting my heart.

One little girl in particular caught my attention. She was shy and stood near the back observing. She saw me look at her and let a little smile show through. I came up to her later and offered a hug, she resisted initially but then held on tight. One of the ladies who works at the home told me her story.

This tiny jewel was born to a family that, for whatever reason, decided since she was born a girl they did not want her to live. They dug her grave, and then covered her with honey and left her on an ant hill to die. By the grace of God she was rescued and taken to this children's home to be cared for. The grave reality struck me. All twenty two of these babies were meant to be dead by their very own families. Thousands more won't get the chance of life like these girls.

As we later sang "Making Melodies" for the second time that day I knew that the King of Kings had to be beaming listening to his prized creations singing songs of praise.

Now as the mother of a daughter, and a second on its way, I couldn't be more thrilled for a chance to mother the daughters of the King. Our little princesses truly are a gift!

Author: Michelle Hanning

Wife to Griff. Mom to two girls. Lover of
missions and especially India.

Not So Different... Really

Haiti.

I had heard its name so many times, but never seriously considered traveling there. It wasn't until the huge earthquake that killed over 220,000 people occurred that it really made me wonder about the country very much.

Two years after the devastation, a team of physicians invited me to join them for a medical trip to Ile de La Gonâve, a Haitian island, to the village of Anse-à-Galets to perform surgeries and visit orphanages. Would there be another earthquake? I got over my fears and thought of the people who have lived there their entire lives.

I wasn't afraid of travel. I had been to 20 countries before Haiti; several of them developing nations. But this time was different. I was asked to dream with people there. To see how their innate creativity, craftsmanship, strengths, and identity could help them out of poverty. I was excited to guide and direct and use my creativity and marketing skills to help. Give them purpose and an avenue for their skills. I wanted to make an impact, to change their lives, give them new hope and purpose, and to make my time there meaningful.

But then differences popped into my mind.

They speak Creole. Their skin tone is much, much darker than mine. They eat different food than I eat. Would they accept me? Listen to my ideas? We're just so different you know.

I assisted in the operating room. A woman came in to have a c-section. It was the first I had ever seen, and as soon as that baby was held up by the doctor, I started crying. I pondered that moment. And then I realized she isn't so different from me. She had the desire to bring forth life. To have children and see them grow. To bring up a new generation in the richness of history and generational blessings.

A woman with years of severe abdominal pain came in for exploratory surgery. She left the OR without a uterus. Her family was shocked, saddened, and dismayed. I knew her tears would freely fall when she woke up. I pondered. And then I realized she isn't so different from me. The inability to have children-a finality to dreams-would be a crushing blow. So much of identity as a woman is being able to be a mother. I felt her pain.

I sat on a wooden bench and some girls started stroking my blonde hair. Soon, I felt a brush on my head. Public health study brought to mind every possible parasite I could acquire. I had to talk myself out of worst-case-scenario thoughts. I glanced up and all of the girls were grinning and laughing, extremely happy. I stopped worrying and happily acquired rows of tight French braids. I pondered. And then I realized they aren't so different from me. The girls want to braid hair and make me look pretty. To show their skills and work as a team to be girly girls. They wanted to share their knowledge with a new friend.

Riding in the back of a rickety pick-up truck to a remote village, we stopped to look at a newly built latrine and water well. Coming down the road was a woman with a chunky, ridiculously cute baby. I cooed and oohed and ahhed, telling her how cute her baby was. To my delight, she handed him over to me. To my surprise, she kept on walking down the road. The public health worker quickly said, "Give the baby back!" I realized that she was prepared to give her baby to me to keep. Forever. I pondered.

And then I realized she isn't so different from me. She already had dreams stored up in her heart for her baby before he was even born. She had hopes for him before he was even conceived. She has a fierce, protective, mother's heart. She knew that she wanted more for her baby than he would likely ever have in life if he were to grow up on Ile de La Gonâve. She was prepared to sacrifice and do what she felt was best for her baby.

Orphans. The word evokes love, compassion, and sympathy. I visited an orphanage with 72 children supported by three hard working women, fed from two wood-fired stoves, where all kids share clothes and shoes. I brought crayons and paper plates-meager offerings-and let them draw and sing songs. As I rose to leave, a little girl wrapped her arms around my leg and started sniffling quietly. Big tears fell down her cheeks. I pondered. And then I realized she isn't so different from me. She wants a family. To belong. To be delighted in as someone's daughter. She wants to be seen as an individual and stop being an orphan, feeling separate, and different. She has dreams of family and what her life could be like...to really be seen.

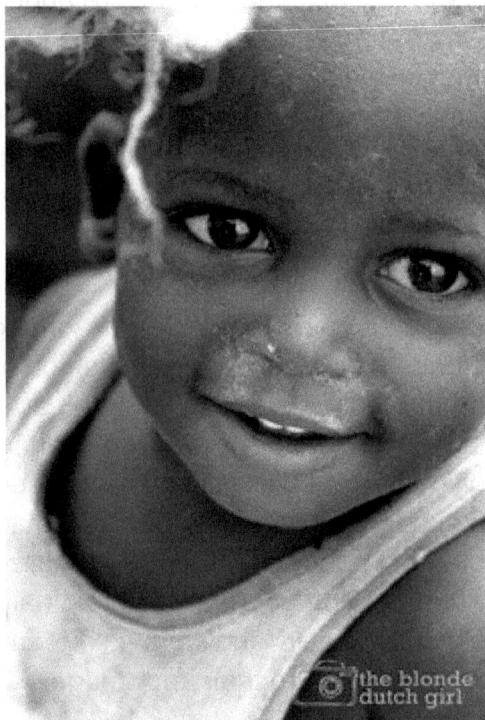

I made my way down to check out the Saline (Salt Flats) and see the ocean. On the way, a little village girl grabbed my hand and smiled up at me. We wound through houses made of sticks and rusty tin. We were surrounded by dozens of giggling, laughing, smiling kids. Some only wore a shirt. All were covered in dusty salt. Fascinated with my camera, they posed and made faces, jumped and danced, played tag and duck, duck, goose. I pondered. And then I realized they aren't so different from me. They want to be filled with joy, to play, to be in community. They want to live in unbridled freedom and take the hand of a trusted adult to walk through life with them.

In those moments of pondering, I realized that we are much more similar than I realized. Truth and desire and hopes and dreams are written on the hearts of people everywhere. We are created with the need to love and be loved and see future generations thrive. In the end, we're not so different...really.

Author: Melissa Tenpas

A photographer, world traveler, editor, athlete, adventurer, marketer, dreamer. Community leader working to redeem and love the brokenhearted. Fascinated with God's amazing world. Welcome to my world.

BlondeDutchGirl.com

Sowing Seeds on Foreign Soil

The four-part harmony flowing down the streets raised curious eyebrows. Not just the singing, but the Charles Dickens' era clothing we wore. My top hat and bulky overcoat stood out among the sophisticated style of the Italian people.

We had a purpose, but I admit I had doubts. How could a naive group of American Bible school students make a difference in a foreign country? We didn't speak the language. We didn't know our way around. We relied heavily upon the missionaries to schedule performances, and then they had to speak to those we serenaded.

Italy was beautiful. I was continually awestruck by its grandeur- the rich history, fascinating architecture, and savory foods. But this wasn't a tour. We'd been trained to spread the gospel to the far reaches of the Earth. And now, on the mission field, I stood bewildered. How could singing Christmas carols to shoppers in the marketplace do anything for God's kingdom? As simple entertainment, how could this permanently affect eternity?

Then one evening, at the most unexpected time, God showed me.

A young man in the local church was part of a group of dancers... break dancers. All the guys in our group lit up at the opportunity to watch them practice. I'd never seen anything like it. Unbeknownst to me, God had a plan. A man in his early twenties approached us and asked the missionary who we were. I didn't understand a word of her explanation but watched as the man sat on the floor at her feet and talked with her for an hour. She explained later that she'd told him we were Christians and here to proclaim the love of Jesus. He had many questions about God, and as the practice continued behind him, she answered each one.

I sat in silence after she told me, fighting back the tears. If all the money I'd raised, time spent memorizing music, and effort to travel that far was all so one man could hear about Jesus, it was worth it. I'd been so arrogant to think that God had to speak through me to be included in his plan. But a young Italian was told the gospel simply because I was there.

And God wasn't done.

I watched through new eyes now as I sang. Waiting. Waiting to see God touch somebody else. As I hugged the elderly in a nursing home, most cried because they appreciated somebody caring about them. The gospel simply shared through acts of love.

As we sang in the marketplace the missionary passed out literature to those watching. I smiled as I saw a passerby thumb through the Gospel of John.

I'd learned in school that God raises some to plant seeds and others to harvest. I realized we were the seed planters. God had planned for me to be in Italy that Christmas, and though I lacked the faith, God accomplished what he'd set out to do.

Two years later, I returned. Same mission, same location. But this time, I anticipated what God would do. We had a purpose. And I had no doubts. God was there. God was active. He would use us in unexpected and glorious ways.

Author: Joshua McNeal

He loves to combine the power of the Gospel with the power of storytelling. A simple man sharing simple stories of not-so-simple truths.

JoshuaJMcneal.com

What God Thinks About You

"So, where are you headed?" I asked the young brunette next to me to end the awkward silence. She smiled the stranger smile, as if wondering how long this conversation might take. "Somewhere tropical. With friends." She needed a little prodding, and I wondered if I should just lay off. Instead, I offered my own less glamorous destination: Atlanta.

I attempted to stir the conversation with more questions about her destination, responding with appropriate amounts of awe and jealousy. I hoped we would catch a common thread in our lives and the chatter would take off, giving me an opportunity to eventually talk with her about Jesus.

But no such luck. The conversation flailed, and we politely took up our books. I leaned into the window, pretending to read, but inside I argued with myself, knowing God might have bigger plans for this three-hour plane ride.

Eventually, my discomfort with silence grew larger than my desire to be well-mannered company. "What are you reading?" I finally inquired. She stammered a bit. "It's a little unconventional. I'm not sure I want to say." She tucked the pink book cover down toward her lap. I attempted to reassure her I didn't have plans to judge, but I wasn't going to push it. But what was she reading?

"I'm reading about artificial insemination," she offered hesitantly, waiting for the verdict to read on my face as she turned the cover toward me. "I'm not married yet, but I'm 35. And I want to have a baby."

Oh.

I can't remember what I said next. Keeping my poker face straight while managing my inner Morality Police turned into a full-time job. What about the child with a father he never knows? You need to address this. You can't just act like sin isn't sin, the Police huffed.

Easy for you to say, my rational side sassed back. You're married with a child. Just listen. There's a reason she's choosing this.

"So where are you in the deciding process?" I queried, trying to appear open-minded but hoping she picked the book up at Barnes and Noble last week.

"I've decided to do it," she answered resolutely, gaining confidence now that the secret was out. "I'm in the early stages of preparation, taking prenatals. Selecting a donor. That's the hard part."

I could only imagine.

I wrestled with my convictions, but I knew an ultra-conservative rant would immediately end the conversation. Besides, with the extent of my knowledge being Jennifer Aniston's movie, The Switch, I couldn't really articulate my beliefs on this topic anyway. So I opted for empathy, the kind of listening that sits down next to you, tucks its knees to its chest, and cries in all the right spots.

I asked more questions about her journey and discovered she looked into adoption, but no agencies allowed a single woman to adopt in her state. So here she was, 35 years old and single, her biology staring impatiently at its watch. It made sense from her perspective. Artificial insemination was the only empowered choice left.

She never envisioned life this way, she added, implying, if a man wasn't going to come around and stay, what else could she do?

Our conversation lulled again, and she returned to her book. In the quiet roar of the plane, I listened again. This time to God. I asked what he thought about her, what was really going on. I asked him to speak to the real issue, not the political-moral issue of artificial insemination, but the reason behind the reason. And he did.

That quiet voice I'm learning to hear spoke of the hope she used to know, but after so many disappointments, she lost its brightness from her eyes. He gently shared her worth and value, and what he wanted to give back to her. I sat with my pen and scribbled it all down, filled with compassion as I listened to a lovesick Father speak of his beloved daughter.

As I listened in to heaven in my window seat, the moral problem became a person again.

The plane began its descent into Atlanta, and my heart raced. I had to time it perfectly to tell her what God said without leaving too much possible sitting uncomfortably next to each other. Because what if she thinks I'm crazy?

As the ground rushed up to meet us, I turned to her. "I know this might sound funny, but I was just asking God what he thinks about you. Would you like to know what he said?"

Her countenance softened, brows raised. "Sure." I didn't expect this response.

As I shared with her what I heard, the faraway God came close. She nodded in agreement as I spoke, and I knew I really had heard God. As I handed her the paper with my notes, she smiled wide. "This week is starting off really well. I've got some things to think about."

My inner Pharisee sulked a bit, not having the chance to correct the errant behavior. But Jesus looked on proud. Rather than choosing to address the "Right Vs Wrong", I listened for the story *under* the story and let God speak to the hurt and longing aching beneath.

If God can treat a woman who doesn't know him yet with such dignity, how much does he also want to meet me in my disgrace and disappointment? Indeed, this is how he draws all of us to himself, telling us the truth of who we are, erasing shame, resurrecting hope.

Author: Sarah Siders

Sarah Siders is a social working writer launching a church plant with her husband. She writes on parenting, relationships and being a human following Jesus at her blog.

SarahSiders.com

Redefining Childhood

Squeezed together on the bench seat of an old van, Speciose and I couldn't help knocking into each other as we bounced over potholes, swerved around pedestrians crowding the red clay roads of Kigali, Rwanda.

She speaks Kinyarwanda to someone on her cell phone, clothed in vibrant African dress, hair braided like a piece of art. I only know one language and this woman, living in a third world country, can speak four. I am one of several visiting Americans shifting through her world, fascinated by her skill in translation and bartering.

We eat lunch at separate tables on a crowded terrace overlooking the metal roof skyline of the city. I notice a faraway look; she picks at her food quietly. It leaves me curious.

On my last day in Rwanda, during a final embrace she reveals what haunts her. "The children are starving and we have no way to feed them. Do you think you can help," she asks hesitantly.

We stare at each other seriously, then break the silence with a giggle when she tells me her five year old daughter doesn't understand why she can't bring all the orphans home with her.

I accept the challenge and together, over five years, we manage to help sustain eighty children –orphaned in the genocide and living in a village of child-headed households. Her courageous question is the seed for our blooming friendship; the soil for a community fund raising effort championed by my local church.

On my second journey back to Rwanda, Speciose and I push our way through crowd- filled tents, walking serpentine around fresh market tables, avoiding eye contact with eager business owners greedy for muzungu (white man) money. A woman preaches the Gospel loudly, proclaiming Christ through a crude speaker.

"You look smart," remarks a shop owner. She refers to my long traditional dress, handmade by a fastidious Rwandan tailor. I respond with a smile, clump the skirt in my fists, hiking it above my feet to navigate over heaps of green bananas lying on the dirt floor.

English potatoes, chunky carrots, and heads of cabbage rivaling the size of my own fill white cloth sacks standing as tall as my teenage son. Hoisted on the backs of frail young men, they are carried to the cab of our pickup truck already loaded with toilet paper, salt, soap, and kerosene; luxuries we're transporting to the orphans for my first trip to Hope Village. I'm startled to learn that toilet paper will be a first in the community; Speciose tells me the children use outdated magazine pages.

A cloud of dust shadows behind us on the bumpy uphill ride, flagging our arrival. As red clay powder settles into every crevice and blankets the windshield, I notice the outlines of silhouettes seated in a windowless building before us, their new community space maturing in stages of construction as we raise funds. The children are gathered and patiently waiting for the arrival of the faceless Americans who help them.

When I move in close enough to see the whites of their eyes, I'm shocked. They are no longer children orphaned in genocide, but young adults. Time scabs over their wounds, leaving their stories less tender. Several stand up for an embrace and allow me the grace of an interview.

We meet inside one of their houses, the size of a walk-in closet. I prop up a voice recorder on the ledge of a hole in the mud wall referred to as a window, face each subject as sweat drips down my back and push the play button. One by one, I ask through an interpreter about their past; why they ended up in the village and how they would describe their life since. I'm not sure any of us were prepared to hear their answers.

How does one sift through the horror of images of entire families mutilated and then go on to forgive their perpetrators?

As they describe being children captured, beaten, raped, pillaged and wandering as orphans during the 1994 genocide, I offer silent prayers that revisiting the trauma won't peel off the scabs on their wounds. The depth of their suffering swells in my throat. Some were learning to walk when left to fend for themselves with no one to bathe them, put a Band-Aid on a cut, prepare a well-rounded meal, or tuck them in at night.

But redemption dissolves the lump. Stories of gratitude break open places of displaced wonder as they describe thankfulness amidst such an atrocity. Their sense of belonging found in the

Village setting them free to love, and receive it once again. Desperation transforms to hope through the loving embrace of a heavenly Father expressed in community. And suddenly, what I think I need radically changes.

I wipe tears from my face, remember Speciose's daughter and understand more fully the way she thinks. I want to bring them all home with me too. And perhaps I have. Their voices on my recorder remind me what it means when Jesus says, "Come to me as little children, the Kingdom of heaven belongs to such as these." (Matthew 19:14)

Author: Shelly Miller

Shelly Miller is a writer, photographer, clergy wife, and mother of teens who enjoys writing stories that make people think differently about life.

RedemptionsBeauty.com

Only the Beginning

I will never forget the first time I rode into Mexico. I was in between 8th and 9th grade and this was my first time leaving the States. I remember feeling nervous as we waited in line in our 15 passenger van at the border crossing. The officials were intimidating and we held our breath with serious faces until they gave the green light. While our van crossed over from Texas into the border town of Reynosa I eagerly looked out the window and began to absorb the sights and sounds of this new place I was in. The ride from the border to the children's home where we would stay was short but is something that was etched into my 13 year old mind.

The first thing I noticed after crossing the border into Mexico was the smell. It wafted into our air conditioned van and all 12 of us grew quiet as we realized our perceptions were now being forever changed. We drove along the streets of this unfamiliar country and I saw something I haven't ever forgotten. Along the side of the rode were cardboard boxes with slats of tin covering the top. People stared out at us; some with curiosity, some their eyes empty. In one of these makeshift shelters was a little boy just barely 2 years old with large dark eyes. The only thing that covered his little body was a diaper. He sat in the dirt floor. His face filthy along with the rest of him and the tin shelter, his home.

There are moments in life that shape you, change you, and for me this was the first of many. My borders had expanded, my world had enlarged, and my heart had grown. That trip was the first for me but by no means the last. To Mexico, Guatemala, Ukraine. Hundreds of beautiful children, with bright eyes and dirty faces stole my heart. These trips changed the course of my life and impacted who I have become, who I am becoming.

The little boy in the shelter. The family who dusted off old paint buckets for us to sit on while they spent what little money they had on a bottle of cold Coca Cola for us, their guests. The little girl playing in the shade and dirt underneath a church. The children without parents. The homes built between piles of garbage, their neighborhood the city dump. Little hands holding onto long sticks clinging to a bridge asking for money, for food. A dirty river, the only water source.

All of these moments made me realize step by step, year by year that my reality is not really reality at all for the majority of the world. Once I realized what the world truly was made up of I no longer could look away and remain unchanged.

These moments, these pictures that flash across my mind aren't only from over the border or across the sea. In my mind I see people standing in long hot lines for a bottle of cold water after a storm and a flood in New Orleans. I see necklaces created by caring, loving hands. Hands that are trying to save a home that is being taken by water in Iowa. There is a woman with a homeless sign thanking me for my small offer of trail mix in Minneapolis. I hear a tear-filled voice lift up prayers for family members lost and lives broken. I shed tears for young women sharing stories of innocence stolen in dark places.

Every time I allow my eyes and heart to be opened to this reality, I know I am once again changed. This is where faith moves from belief to action, talk begins to fuel a cause and people cannot be kept silent or motionless. It started in a van filled with Jr. Highers on it's way to Mexico. But that was only the beginning and I have a feeling I am nowhere near the end.

Author: Stephanie Page

Stephanie is a wife and mom to 3. Her heart is to see people living their lives on purpose for the glory of God. She spends her time as a speaker, writer, bible study leader and conference planner.

StephanieMPage.com

No Uniform Routine

I opened the closet door with a sigh and removed the uniform from its hanger. Those red and white stripes made me cringe as they always did. For a self-proclaimed fashionista like me I dreaded putting it on. When I reached Holy Cross Hospital, Sister Ceciliana had a new kind of assignment for me. This week, the candy striper volunteers would be visiting with patients in the long term care wing instead of running the usual errands of delivering notes or welcoming guests at the information booth.

I made my way down the long underground corridor that emerged on the opposite side of the hospital. "Hola, Amber!" I was welcomed by the cheerful nurse on the floor where I was assigned. "My name is Elsa, and I will be in my office down the hall if you need anything. You can start by saying hello to the young man in room 102. His name is Michael."

Nothing could have prepared me for what I saw. Machines echoed obnoxious sounds that vibrated throughout the room, tubes twisted every which way covering the boy's body, and pictures of a smiling Michael with his family members graced the tables and walls. The lights flickered dimly, and there on the bed lay Michael. Hair shaved, struggling to grow over his forehead, mouth twisted in an unnatural grin, his bony arms curved backwards. A small puddle of drool oozed from his mouth and he stared blankly towards a window.

Not sure what to do I took a seat and began to read to him from my Bible. I made as much small talk as I could with someone who was not able to respond, but my mind wandered. "That could be me. I'm 16 too." I couldn't stop staring at the vibrant images of Michael with his friends in the pictures around me.

"How could this happen so suddenly?" I agonized. "He looked so healthy". Nearly half an hour went by before I said, "Thanks Michael, for listening to me today. I'll be back next week." I tried to sound cheerful, but my voice wavered.

Later that day I did the rest of my rounds playing gin and chatting with mostly elderly patients. It was rare to have someone as young as Michael in this part of the hospital. As I drove home in the family van and parked it in the driveway tears fell.

Before, my job was just a way to get hours in volunteering for school credit. But now, it meant much more to me than that. I would want someone to be with my son or daughter as they lay in a hospital bed. I would want someone to keep them company, to show them some compassion, and give their existence meaning.

Sitting there with Michael in a smelly hospital room was one of the most uncomfortable moments of my life but I will never forget it. That encounter reminded me that life is brief and meant to be cherished. God doesn't abandon us in our suffering. He sends those who need us just as much as we need them.

Throwing the car keys into a basket by the front door I went to my room and changed out of my uniform. Normally, I would toss it aside or leave it crumpled on the floor. But this time I took that red and white striped uniform and gently hung it on a hanger. My hand lingered there for a moment. As I closed the door to my closet I realized that a new door had opened to the way I look at life.

Author: Amber Lia

A Southern California girl, Amber writes and blogs while partnering with her husband as faith-friendly TV and Film producers. She is writing her first book and loves raising her three young sons.

MotherofKnights.com

Sarah, The Least Likely Entrepreneur

Once upon a time, I was born in the small town of Peculiar, Missouri. "How strange," you say - and you would be right. I was firstborn to a pretty great family. My childhood was filled with summer's spent out-of-doors, cut-off from television and air conditioning; spent instead rummaging around a creek somewhere or fort-building in the back yard.

On the rare occasion that television was on the docket I can remember watching those child-sponsorship-style commercials with little African babies, bellies all distended, flies forever stuck in the corners of their eyes and thinking in my 10-year-old mind 'Why is this happening?'

This seemed to develop into a theme over the next few years and I eventually found myself studying the memoirs of activists and pioneers within the justice realm such as Mother Teresa, Ghandi, and Desmond Tutu. I was fascinated with radical living - I think mostly because of a deeply rooted fear of living a mediocre life. These leaders challenged me because they were so completely SOLD OUT in loving others at their own expense, challenging us to give not only out of excess, but out of our poverty as well.

I knew I wasn't there yet.

So my junior year of college I committed to spending the year after I graduated overseas.

The following September I embarked on an eight-month journey around the globe to do my idealistic best to "change the world" alongside two like-minded young women. I think my mother started coloring her hair that year as her eldest traveled to East Africa for five months, then on to Thailand and Cambodia, completing the journey with a partially solo hitchhike through Australia and New Zealand. During that time I called home exactly once, just before spending Christmas on top of Kilimanjaro.

That adventure was the third most life-changing event of my now 31 years. I wrestled with my belief in a good God. I struggled with the lack of human response to poverty. I wept each day as I watched beautiful Thai women selling their bodies to paunchy European men in festive Hawaiian shirts. I wrestled hard and came home a good deal skinnier, sporting a tatty t-shirt, worn-out Chacos, and a pervasive peace.

Three years later, I crossed the ocean a second time with a husband fresh off the altar and a couple of 18-year-old kids from Colorado. We spent about a month in East Africa, and it was there that I met the young Ugandan man that would inspire me to help start businesses around the world.

Soon after our return, my friend Donavan and I found ourselves becoming reacquainted over a cup of coffee, discussing a shoebox full of bamboo jewelry and a business card from a local social enterprise. The bamboo jewelry was supposed to help fund a youth club in Jinja, and Dave and Morgan of Light Gives Heat were going to teach us how. This sweet couple spent hours on the phone answering our legal-pad-worth of questions (did I mention Donavan and I have one intro-to-business course between us?) and then allowed us to consign some of their beautiful Ugandan paper beads to help us get going.

Some high school students bought us a pop-up tent and a friend lent us some tables and there we were, in business. A summer's worth of farmer's markets allowed us to buy into 2 other freedom initiatives, expanding our line and adding to our stores.

Astonishingly, it began to grow. And in the process I developed an incredible love for our artisans globally, as well as a deep gratitude toward our volunteers and supporters. I also gained less-fulfilling relationships with the Secretary of State, the Department of Revenue, Liability Insurance, and a very nice non-profit lawyer named Dustin. At the end of the day, however, we were able to open a brick-and-mortar in Colorado Springs with a really fun product line made justly all around the world. We now conduct business trainings on three continents and watch as people are empowered to create change within their own lives and communities through equitable trade.

Oh my eyes still glaze over when people (aka my husband) start talking about profit-and-loss statements, Quickbooks, and search engine optimization. Tax time is literally the darkest fourteen days of my year.

Really, when it comes down to it, I have none of the typical skills required to run a business. Twelve times a day I think to myself, "now who can I get to do that for me?" Not because I don't want to do it, but because I'm just not altogether equipped.

That's where the joy of partnership comes in. We are so loved by so many, and those friends give us their time and talents to make us much more than we could be otherwise.

So be encouraged, because that old American adage "Follow Your Dreams" is true! At the risk of sounding a bit like I'm touting rainbows and butterflies, if someone like ME can run a business, YOU can build a building, be a famous actor, or raise amazing kids. Most of us were born in the land of opportunity for goodness' sake. It would be a shame to waste all of that free education.

Even those of us struggling with deep opposition still have access to clean water, emergency medical care, a-not-entirely-corrupt government, and social services. We are all created to do something so specific that the world will lack if we don't do just that.

So please, do what you are made to do! If I have learned anything from four years of unlikely entrepreneurship, it is that ideas are a dime a dozen, but few are they with the courage to act on them. Those of us who do need only begin to put one foot in front of the other, and ask for help along the way.

Remember: to whom much has been given, much is required. Great risk can lead to great reward!

Author: Sarah Ray

I am a happily married, mountain-loving, tea-drinking visionary, motivated by the love of Jesus and the hope of seeing captives set free through business and equitable trade.

Yobelinternational.org

Real Love is an Action

She walked up the street in her too tight, too short, skirt. She was moving quickly and he was behind her barking orders... "get over there. Don't lose him."

When I saw her something compelled me to try and stop her. I ran to walk along side her and awkwardly mumbled something about how Jesus loved her, and invited her to a free meal at the church two blocks over next Sunday.

Faint words that felt hollow.

She tried to dismiss me. He was always there barking at her in sort of an urgent whisper. I insisted that she take the paper I was handing out. She didn't look at me, but quickly took the paper to quiet me. She said "thanks" and I let her walk away.

I looked longingly after her for a while wondering what I could do to reach her. How could I help her. How could I tangibly show her Christ's love? She is forever burned in my mind.

She was a prostitute and I was a fresh faced college girl from a small town who decided that I was going to make a difference in the inner city... with or without anyone's help.

A few months earlier I was in my room at college upset by a story I had just read about inner-city kids who had done some horrible violent thing. I remember praying (rather haughtily) "Lord, they just need to know your love. Someone needs to show them your love."

Nearly immediately I felt the Holy Spirit answer back saying "Kari, will you show them my love?"

My heart fell into my stomach. Who me? What? I can't! They wouldn't listen to me!

Several months later, not really knowing what I was doing and to the horror of my parents, I connected with a couple of churches in downtown Seattle, moved into an apartment next to one of them and began to walk the streets at night talking to people about God.

One of my first encounters was this woman. The prostitute. I didn't feel good about our encounter and I kept replaying it over and over in my mind. How in the world was I going to 'SHOW them' his love? I came to realize that our encounter had been all about me! I had no concept of where she was coming from and I was trying to tell her what she needed. This was not showing her the love of Christ! This was showing superiority!

I began to watch what other Christians were doing. Many were standing on the street corner loudly proclaiming that "unless they turned they were all going to burn in hell." I was embarrassed for them. Loudly proclaiming the wages of sin without sharing God's free grace. That wasn't showing them the love of Christ. That was condemnation.

From that moment on I vowed I was going to do this "street witnessing" thing different. I prayed for insight.

I walked the streets looking for a way to reach them while drug deals went on, prostitutes offered themselves, people had sex in the alleyways, and young runaway girls tried to live. People. People God created. People God knows intimately. People he loves.

God placed compassion on my heart for them and I decided I would do something radical. Something no one else was doing. I decided I would just talk to them and see what God did with it. No plan of sharing the gospel, no plan of how to corner them into accepting Christ, just talk to them.

So as I walked the street I would find someone and say. "Hi, I'm out here trying to see what other people believe about God. Can you tell me what you believe? Is there a God, and what does that look like to you?"

It's interesting what happens when you talk to people like real human beings. They become real human beings. I never had anyone shove me away, or scoff at me. They actually talked to me.

Here I was, a completely typical college girl on the streets with some of the scariest looking, most counter-culture, and worst-off people you can imagine just having a conversation.

I loved hearing peoples answers to my question. Their tone was usually mixed with a bit of apprehension, waiting for me to attack their ideas. But I only asked more questions to deeper understand their belief. Which drew them out further, and almost every time they then asked me what I believe. This gave me an open door to say....

"I believe that God created each one of us individually and for a unique purpose. I believe that he loves us so much that he was willing to forgive us anything so he could have a relationship with us. I believe that Jesus died and rose from the grave forever paying for our wrong and giving us freedom. I believe that freedom is for anyone who will accept it."

Words they listened to. Words they heard because they saw that they were accepted right where they were. Words they thought about because I listened to them first.

God called me off my couch and into the world to show me that it's not enough to tell people what's right in God's eyes. We must show them. Real love is an action.

"Faith if it is not accompanied by action is dead" James 2:17

Author: Kari Day

Kari Day is a wife and mom of three. Her passion is to live the purposeful life God has called her to right in the midst of her ordinary everyday and help other women do the same.

KariDay.com

Throw Up Your Hands

I was a married college student racing to work and thinking about class afterward. Every penny counted and it was daylight about 8:30 am, so I parked in the free lot a distance behind the building where I worked. As my left foot exited the car, I found myself blocked by a man. I felt something was wrong, but he just asked me for the time. As I looked down at my watch, he put his hands around my throat and dove into the car.

Somehow, I was forced from a seated position in the driver seat of my Ford Escort, to my knees of the passenger floorboard in seconds. I have no recollection of the struggle. I had been beaten in the process and was now facing the passenger seat.

Scripture says that since we know not what we ought to pray for, the Holy Spirit intercedes for us with groans that words cannot express (Romans 8:26; I Corinthians 14:2). That is what happened as I began to pray loudly in words that were not my own.

With frustration, he yelled, "What are you doing?"

I responded, "Praying."

"Shut up!"

I continued loudly praying.

"Stop it!"

I said, "I can't " and I continued.

This bizarre interaction continued as we drove for about 45 minutes allowing me to consider the possible outcomes. Taking an injury with hopes of being found would be better than being kidnapped and disappearing. From the floor I could only see slightly through the window. I tried to determine his driving pattern and convinced myself that I could throw the door open and jump when he slowed down. I came so close, but when I mustered some courage to do so he drove the car into a field of four feet high grass and stopped.

"Get out!" he said.

I threw the door open and sprinted as fast as I could down the path left by the car. I was not going to look back. I heard him running behind me, and then I was tackled. After struggling on the ground, he ended up on top of me with both hands on my throat strangling me. I was fighting for my life!

The Bible teaches of separate spiritual and physical worlds but we rarely see them. We are provided with stories of angels visiting, God speaking audibly, Christ's presence, and the Holy Spirit providing an inner knowing or direction during prayer. But I never expected it to apply to me.

As I was physically fighting I experienced the most calm peaceful presence I have ever known before or since. And although I did not physically see or hear him, I believed that Christ was standing next to my head as I struggled on the ground. It was as if I could reach out and touch his feet.

Then in my spirit we conversed as follows while physically I fought:

"So this is how I am going to die" very calmly, accepting, and as a statement of fact, not with alarm.

I made an appeal that I wanted to improve certain relationships before I died, but still not concerned about dying. His presence confirmed an afterlife with him and I was at peace.

Christ responded, "You are not going to die (today). THROW UP YOUR HANDS. "

It was a direction firmly stated and quickly accepted.

It was completely counter intuitive and my typical response would be to debate, argue, and ask for confirmation. No time, I threw my hands up in response yet without a clue what would happen.

My attacker had continued to choke me the entire time. However, with me struggling he was unable to cut off my windpipe. When I threw my hands over my head, my attacker briefly continued to choke me. And then he just stopped!

The intense presence of Christ that I described was gone. But I had assurance that I would live through this ordeal. I was lying on my left side with my attacker sitting on my waist catching my breath. Both of us appeared to think, "What next?"

My attacker pulled me off the ground and dragged me to the driver side of the car. I had never thought of a potential rape until that moment. Empowered with the knowledge that I was not going to die and how God was with me was a "Game Changer". I did not know how but I was certain the dynamics had changed.

I will never know my attacker's intent. I was pushed into the driver seat and he ran around to the passenger seat and then ordered, "Lay back the car seat." With our faces only inches apart, I said, "Jesus is Lord, don't you know that!" In my heart I yelled it. In truth, I heard my squeaking shaking voice make the statement. You should have seen the shock on his face! I did not know if he was crazy but I suspected at that point he thought I was. He appeared disappointed he was not in control as intended. He took my wallet and threatened he had my ID and knew where I lived and worked. He ran away.

Sadly the police documented the assault as a burglary since our laws are easier to enforce for property rights. I accidentally overheard the detectives speaking while fingerprinting my car and taking my picture "she should be dead". One concerned officer apologized that I heard them, "I am sorry, but these things don't typically end this way."

I am now thankful for the event so that when my Christianity is not convenient or challenging I cannot dismiss what God has done for me. After that day I've encountered numerous events when God reminds me to "throw up your hands" and cast my cares to him. When I submit and rely on him, the outcome has always been something beyond what I could have imagined. I am still learning this truth.

Author: Cindy Cooper

I am married and live with my family in Texas. I have worked for 25+ years as a CPA in industry. I am learning to share my faith more and was asked to give my testimony.

Beauty From Ashes, One Day at a Time

November 6, 2010 was the beginning of the end for my mom. Her cancer was aggressive, and on that morning mom woke up unable to speak or write. That day we discovered there were 3 tumors on her brain. In those moments life changed for me.

In the months that would follow leading up to the passing of my mom depression walked through new doors in my life, sin crept into the corners of my heart, anxiety beat within the walls of my chest, and sometimes darkness threatened to take my life. Yet through all of that I have been able to overcome the unknown and hold onto the hand of my Creator, my God, to allow Him to turn me into beauty from ashes.

Mom held on for 4 months after that horrible day of discovering the tumors. I held on too, but barely by a thread. My husband had lost his job in the midst of that deadly diagnosis. I was mom's caregiver, second to my dad, and I was desperately striving to function. Those months were dark for me. I felt more alone than I ever had. I didn't know how to share the desperation with those around me, so I often held it in, allowing barriers to go up. Mom went home to be with the Lord on March 20, 2011. I never thought that my life would be the same after losing my mom. To be quite honest, it hasn't been. I have traversed ugly paths and chosen unwisely at times.

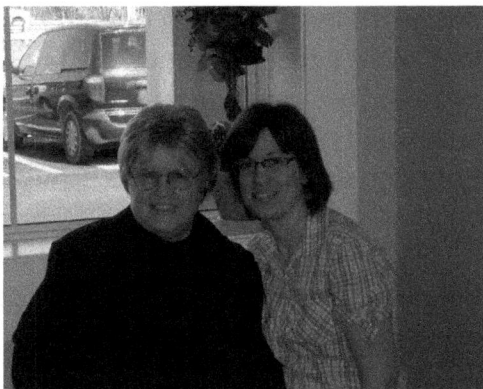

But God walked alongside me the whole way, never leaving me. And now, 2 years later, I am able to see His beauty through what was my ashes. I have seen good come out of this exhausting event. It just took time, prayer, faith, counseling, and healing.

Losing my mom has been one of the ugliest events through which I ever walked. Grief was a long journey for me and took me on some dark routes. Saying goodbye was a long winter season for me. However, in patience and perseverance, I have been able to see how God can use that for His good.

Born out of losing my mom, I took on a cause. We formed the Linda A. Ferguson Memorial scholarship, to be given out to students studying to be oncology nurses. We desired to have mom's name carried on, but even more than that, to have students carry God's light to dark places. Places I had walked myself. Places I couldn't go, but I could help students who could help more cancer patients and families. We fuel funds into mom's scholarship through a 5K, a running event. Running is a passion of mine, it helped me through some of those dark days. Running would help me overcome hurt by bringing good. Giving out that first scholarship in 2012 became a life defining moment for me. My heart was filled in a new way, yet I felt speechless as I tried to put into perspective what seeing the life of that scholarship was like for me.

It brought on waves of new emotion as I remembered my mom by having a scholarship in her memory. Knowing she'd love the girl who was receiving it, missing mom and wishing she were here for it all, but also realizing if I hadn't lost her the scholarship would not even exist was emotional. Seeing good come out of a bad life situation.

Seeing the scholarship and the 5K event unfold brought on more dreams, and brought on the realization that I would carry on. I would be ok. Good came from the bad. Beauty rose up from ashes.

I do not think I will ever be able to say I am thankful I lost my mom. I miss her with a deep heartache and tears more often than not. I can say, however, that I am thankful for all that God is teaching me in the process, for the scholarship we have seen come to life, for a deeper understanding of God's grace and compassion, and for learning to live life one day at a time because it is so short.

Depression still plagues me, but God's compassion covers me. My eyes were opened up to the sin crevices in my heart and God's grace surrounds me. Grief has become peace. And love has found new depths in my life on a daily basis.

He is able to bring beauty from ashes, one day at a time. I am living proof of that.

Author: Rachael McKinney

Wife. Mommy. Barista. Blogger. Runner. Reader. Jesus Lover. Always working on my marriage and my walk with Jesus. Perfectly imperfect and I embrace that.

JavaJogger.blogspot.com

The Empty Chair

I felt called, once, to visit an acquaintance at a local hospital where he was receiving inpatient psychiatric care. I'd never visited this part of the hospital before so I didn't really know what to expect. I'd spoken with a mutual friend who hadn't particularly encouraged my going; he'd visited and didn't feel as though he'd blessed or helped.

Still, I felt called to go.

I told my husband. He--being the cautious, protective sort wasn't especially thrilled with the idea. But, to his credit, he trusted and offered to drive me. He waited in the minivan with Cade and Clementine while I walked in the hospital, wearing maternity overalls.

My acquaintance had provided me the information I needed to receive access, so a nurse at the front desk unlocked the door to the visiting area. There were people everywhere: some sitting on sofas and chairs, others just sort of milling around.

I'd assumed I'd have to wait for my acquaintance to join me, but to my surprise I saw he was already sitting in the visiting area. He was talking with two other men at a small, square table.

The chair just to the left of my acquaintance was the only empty chair in the room.

I don't think I have words to tell you how I felt seeing that empty chair. I'd already felt confident that God was calling me to that place. But when I saw the empty chair, the only empty chair, beside my acquaintance, who hadn't known when I'd be visiting, my heart was flooded with joy! There may as well have been a shaft of light pouring into that chair; I knew it was my chair. I knew it was waiting for me: that I was the person meant to fill it.

It was a very humbling, satisfying, overwhelming moment in my spiritual journey and one I pray to never forget.

My acquaintance hugged me and introduced me to his friends, and I sat down in my chair. A pack of cards rested on the table, and I asked the men if they'd like a fourth for spades. We proceeded to play, and I played well thanks to the countless "wasted" hours I'd spent playing the game in college.

With the pressure for eye contact diminished conversation flowed easily and well among us. Before I left I asked if I might lead us in prayer; we joined hands and bowed; and God gave me words.

I don't share this story because I think I did something profound for my acquaintance that day. I share it because God did something profound for me.

If you're anything like me, at least once in your life, you've felt called or compelled to do something, and you've talked yourself out of it. You've told yourself: I'm not the best person for this job. I'm ill-equipped. There's someone better.

And you know what? You haven't been wrong, entirely. Because there's always someone better, more experienced, more polished, and less bumbling.

Never-the-less, God doesn't make mistakes. When He calls you to do something His reasons likely have as much, or more, to do with you than with anyone else. He wants to grow and teach you. He has a perfect plan for your life.

So just go: even if your hands shake, your knees knock, and you're at a loss of what to say. Everything will be okay.

God's already in that place to which He's calling you, and He's preparing it (him? her?) for your arrival. Go. Find your empty chair.

Author: Brandee Shafer

Brandee Shafer is an English instructor turned SAHM to the 4 children for whom she records her life and thoughts, through blogging. She and her family live in a log cabin near Richmond, Virginia.

BrandeeShafer.blogspot.com

Serve the Least of These

This stirring in my heart to serve others has been a longtime companion.
It's a stirring waiting to be awakened.

Along my journey the stirring was felt.
I'd see, but never stopped.

Married to a once verbally abusive and alcoholic husband -
Serve the battered and abused women of our world.

Lost in a world of depression and an eating disorder -
Serve those who are also lost.

A heart full of pain -
Serve those drowning in pain.

Wife and mother to military men -
Serve those who serve and protect us.

Rescued and given a new life -
Bring Christ to the lost and hurting souls.

I had always silently cried to be seen.
For far too long I remained unseen.

And this is where the stirring to serve ignites.
"Beth, see those silent cries of others."

Fear left me frozen and feeling powerless.

Bravery was needed to move.

Doubt told me I was unable to make a difference.
Someone else will do it better.

Comfort kept me on my side of the street.
I don't belong on the other side.

But there is so much more on the other side.
There is a hurting world
waiting to be seen.

There he was; this
homeless veteran.
I've seen him again and
again.

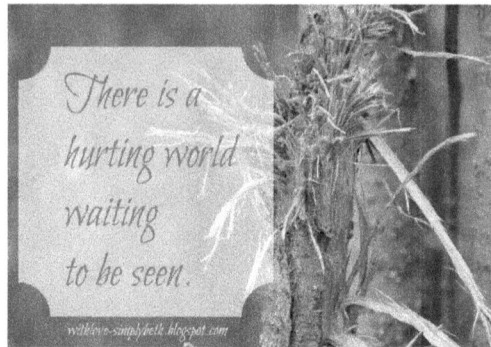

This time I stopped.
I stepped over my fears.

To the other side of the street I went.
I sat down next to Bob and placed my hand on his.

I prayed with my new friend.
"I love you, Beth", he said as we parted ways.

I crossed back over to my side of the street.
Now I long to go back to the other side.

I saw Bob.
Bob saw me.

God saw me.

How can I go on not seeing?

"For even the Son of Man did not come to be served, but to serve,
and to give his life as a ransom for many." ~ Mark 10:45

Author: Beth Stiff

I'm a wife and mom to two boys. I love Jesus, family, friends, reading and a hot cup of coffee to begin my day. I love to write and share about how my relationship with Jesus has changed my life.

WithLove-SimplyBeth.blogspot.com

I Know You Are, But What Am I?

"Where do you have the greatest need?"

These are the famous last words of many volunteers. When my wife and I asked this same question at our church in Chicago we suddenly found ourselves working with special needs children.

I use the terms "special needs" and "children" both very loosely. The students in our class ranged from ages 2 to 82, and the needs ranged from mild autism to severe cerebral palsy. The greatest challenge was often trying to figure out who exactly you were working with and what their specific needs were. It didn't matter though, because we had no training in any of them.

One week, which had started much like any other, a new kid walked in. He looked to be 16 or 17 and painfully shy with his head hung low, keeping to himself. My wife immediately urged me, "Dallas, go talk to him."

I finished up what I was working on and made my way to him. His name was Ryan, and in about the first ten minutes of conversation that was as much information as I could obtain. Most questions were answered with one word, or often just a nod. Small talk got painful as I resorted to asking the questions fourth graders ask at the lunch table, just trying to get any response out of him. "Do you like pizza?"… "Do you think puppies are cute?"

To break up the silence I asked if he wanted to play catch. From about 8 feet apart we threw a small Nerf ball back and forth. I then grabbed a milk crate and started having him shoot baskets. All of this was still not entertaining for either of us, though I pretended as I enjoyed it.

As we squeezed every last ounce of fun out of this activity we moved to a table of board games. We ended up locking in on a game of generic Connect Four that managed to keep us engaged for the remaining hour or so of class. I tried my best to lose without being obvious, and he tried his best to win, which he did most of the time.

On the drive home I told my wife that I felt sorry for Ryan. While it was clear he had needs I didn't feel like this class was right for him. He was too old, and too capable to be in there. I knew he felt awkward, and I just wanted him to feel normal. Oh well, better luck next week.

Next week came, just like it always does, but there was no Ryan. "Well, I guess he felt the same way…" I thought to myself. But then something strange happened. About halfway through class, a volunteer woman whom I had seen before but never really knew approached me.

"Are you Dallas?" she asked.

"Yes ma'am. What's up?"

"Last week you played with my son in here, and…"

"Oh, Ryan?" I interrupted. "We had a great time. Where is he today?"

"He had to go back to college," she replied. I'm sure the puzzled look on my face wasn't too hard to judge. "You see, Ryan was not here as a student. He was here to volunteer on his spring break."

"Uh uh uh uh, I uh uh, I…" Can you hear me stuttering frantically? I panicked. I felt the rush of heat to my face like I was pulling a pizza out of the oven. I stumbled over my words trying to explain myself. I tried to tell her what I told my wife on the drive home. I tried to tell her that I didn't think he belonged there. I couldn't spit it all out fast enough. There couldn't possibly be anything in the world worse than mistaking a woman's son for being mentally retarded when he's fully functioning, right?

Nope, it gets worse.

As I panted and spattered off nonsense, she quickly interrupted me. "It's okay," she said.

"It's okay?" I thought…

"It's okay," she continued, "we had to have the same conversation with him about you on the drive home." In case you missed that, let me state it again. They had to have the same conversation with him about me!

"WHAT!?!?!"

Honestly, the rest of that day is a blur in my memory. I have no idea what I told the woman. I may have cursed her. I may have told her thank you. I have no idea. It wasn't until the drive home that evening while telling this horrendous story to my wife that she made the light bulb click on.

"Well, how did you interact with him?" she asked.

I paused for a second, "OH… MY… GOD!!!" It hit me like a ton of bricks. I immediately remembered the conversations about pizza and puppies. I remembered the game where I made him throw a Nerf ball in a basket from 10 feet away, while I cheered him on. "Yay Ryan!" I remembered the hundreds of games of Connect 4 that I intentionally squandered. "Put the red one there!" he must have been thinking.

As I recounted the days events with my wife I eventually had to pull the car over on the side of the highway we were laughing so hard. There's nothing like seeing yourself through somebody else's eyes.

It was a couple of months later that Ryan returned from college for the summer, and came to volunteer again. Neither of us spoke. Neither of us acknowledged our previous misunderstanding. A simple glance said it all.

Since that day I have been completely open to any opportunity to serve in any capacity. Seriously, what worse could happen?

Author: Dallas Owen

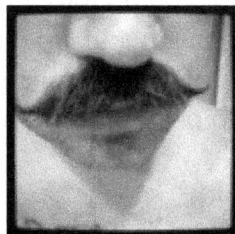

Every year I organize a fundraiser growing mustaches to provide water in Africa through B:WM. I am thrilled to have another avenue to support them. I love Jesus, my wife, 2 kids and hot chicken.

RightintheMustache.com

Wash Their Feet?

There is no natural reason why I should be here. If I had made this decision based on logic or emotion, I would not be in this place right now. I am writing this story while sitting in my hotel room in Phnom Penh, Cambodia. From my [so far] three months here, I can easily think of one hundred reasons why it's uncomfortable. However, I would rather share a story that tells you why it's worth it. While I serve an organization here, my mission is simple: love as many people as I can into the Kingdom through the grace of God. Living this out looks different in every situation, but here is how it appeared when I met Ye Saiya and Ye Vatey.

The two of them walked onto the property with such dignity and grace. Elderly people here in Cambodia have a way of carrying themselves that causes something inside of you to long to respect and honor them. They had come to the church with different ailments, seeking medical treatment from the free clinic. As they sat down to wait in the 'forever' long line my friend and I knelt in front of these frail women to get to know them. As I looked up into the face of Ye Saiya, which bore the marks of a challenging life, I felt as if I was in the presence of royalty. We spent some time getting to know them, and had the opportunity to pray over them.

You need to wash their feet. The thought went through my head and I immediately began thinking of all the reasons why that was a terrible, weird idea. "But God, what if that is not culturally appropriate, what if they are offended, isn't that outdated and slightly cheesy?" I tried with everything inside of me to ignore this blaring idea. I WILL NOT WASH THEIR FEET. I looked at my friend kneeling next to me and quietly said, "I think we're supposed to wash their feet". When she responded saying, "I was just thinking the same thing," I knew there was no way to get out of this. We talked back and forth eliminating all of our pathetic excuses and finally concluded that we should at least ask them if we could wash their feet.

Using a translator to communicate, we asked these beautiful, elderly women if we could wash their feet. My heart was throbbing as I waited for the translator to relay our message, and to hear what their response would be. To my surprise they seemed to receive our request favorably! They gave us their permission to wash their feet! Even still, I was feeling somewhat uncomfortable with the situation. I was certain that everyone there would find it entirely strange that we were washing these precious women's feet, but I knew it was more important to be obedient to God's voice rather than my own selfish fears.

The only water we had was our drinking water, which we were glad to use! Slowly, we began pouring the clean, clear water over their weathered, dirty feet. As the water flowed out from the bottle the tears began to flow from my eyes. Suddenly, it was as if the entire atmosphere had changed. It felt as if Jesus Himself had walked up to us. My heart was overwhelmed by the Father's profound love for these women. When I looked at Ye Saiya's tender face I saw that she too had tears filling her eyes. I did not know what God was doing in her heart, but I knew that it was His moment. The entire scene was more breathtaking than I can begin to capture with words.

Ye Saiya kept saying something in the local Cambodian language, but I was clueless as to what it was. I just kept smiling at her, pointing up, and saying, "Prae Yesu" [Jesus]. The moment came and went, and my heart was filled with the joy that comes from saying "yes" to the beckoning of the Father's heart. Minutes later one of the translators came up to me and explained a beautiful truth.

In Cambodian culture, every New Year, children will wash the head, hands, and feet of their parents as a sign of great honor and respect. Learning this fact alone was a reason for rejoicing, as we knew that what we had done was indeed very honoring to those women. Then my interpreter told me something that overwhelmed my heart to the uttermost. Ye Saiya never had any children to wash her feet. In Cambodia having children is everything. Ye Saiya has lived with the pain and disgrace of never having any children her whole life. Yet in that moment, when I laid down my pride and took the lowest place at her feet, Ye Saiya became a mother and honor was bestowed. What she had been saying to me over and over through tears was, "My daughter, my daughter."

Everything made sense in that moment, and all of my excuses

as to why I didn't want to do it became entirely obsolete. It made me realize that the most wonderful place to be in is the position of simply saying yes to the leading of the Holy Spirit. Though it may be uncomfortable, scary, awkward, etc., when we step out in faith we find that anything that could potentially hold us back no longer has any validity. We are born again to live like Jesus, and Jesus perfectly said yes to the Father every time. He left heaven to dwell amongst us, and took the place of a servant. When we follow His example, and say yes to His leading, we find, therein, a life that is truly abundant. The more we take those opportunities, the more we realize that nothing can hold us back.

*For the sake of privacy, real names have not been used.

Author: Leah Morford

My heart is captivated. I am a girl who loves Jesus recklessly, passionately. I am filled with love, because I have been loved. My ambition in life is to always be a blessing to everyone, everywhere.

Surrendered-Life.blogspot.com

Grace Greater Than Our Sin

"You can't take that in." Standing at the entrance to Phillips State Prison, I tightened the grip on my purse. Clutching that purse made me feel secure, but I reluctantly returned it to the car and entered the gatehouse again.

"Walk through," the guard directed me through the metal detector. "Lift your pants," he said without emotion, sure I'd know what he was talking about.

"Huh?" I asked, as if the confusion on my face didn't say it all. He motioned to the legs of my slacks. "Oh"- realization hit me, and the thought of concealing a weapon made me giggle. What was a thirty-four year old mom doing there?

What was I doing there? I was in prison and you came to visit me. (Matthew 25:36 NIV) While writing a book on how Christ calls us to love our neighbors I found myself inside the steel bars. I wondered how I would write about something I'd never experienced. So in my desperation, I prayed.

God, I want to write about how to reach out to the world around me. I believe an ordinary Christian can change lives. But did you really mean we should visit prisons? If so, Lord, I need help, because I've never even been to one. Does that verse still apply to me today? Help, Lord.

When Dr. W. Dan Parker-or Dr. Dan, as he is known-invited me to join him for a class at Phillips State Prison I knew God was answering my prayer. Of his seventy-one years this man of God has spent fifty-one of them in the ministry. Dr. Dan, a professor at NOBTS (New Orleans Baptist Theological Seminary), had been involved with prison ministry before, but not in this capacity. When the seminary decided to start a ministry degree program at Phillips similar to the one at Angola State Prison in Louisiana, Dr. Dan was asked to teach. He could hardly contain his excitement. "I'm in the business of changing lives," he shared.

I was thrilled but nervous at the invitation. Soon, I was escorted through a series of locked doors. Those behind us would slide shut and lock before the ones in front of us would open. It was a waltz. Step, slide, click. Step, step, slide, click. After the maze of locks I followed Dr. Dan across the campus to the gymnasium, which housed the classrooms. Prisoners walked freely in white jumpsuits. I was surprised, half expecting to see the men in black and white striped uniforms, fastened to balls and chains. I let out a nervous laugh realizing TV formed my every notion of doing time.

When we reached the classroom I prepared to make myself invisible. However, with thirty-one students, the thirty-one desks went all the way to the back wall. "You can sit right here," Dr. Dan pulled an office chair up front within reach of the first desk. "Okay," I drawled, trying to appear relaxed. I was anything but.

Before I could take in a steady breath men poured through the classroom door. I was not prepared for what I saw.

Grace.

Beyond the white jumpsuits, behind the tattoos, above the life sentences, there was grace. As the men were each introduced to me, in their eyes I could see the assurance that only the Holy Spirit brings.

Dr. Dan started class with prayer. They prayed over court dates and death row sentencing. They prayed for the family of a man who was executed only days before. I blinked to make sure I wasn't dreaming. I sat in that room full of thieves, kidnappers and murderers, and the words to an old hymn echoed in my head. "Grace, grace, God's grace,
Grace that will pardon and cleanse within... "

Of the 57,000 men in Georgia's state prison system 31 were chosen for this program. The man on the first row could be my neighbor. He's clean cut, shaven, and he smiled as he leaned forward to share how the Lord led him there. "I wasn't supposed to be here. God brought me. When I applied the lady asked me how I knew about the program. The ads weren't meant to be in my dorm. I told my mom I probably wouldn't get in. But they came in my cell one morning and told me to pack my bags. I made it."

Dr. Dan asked me to share about the book I'm writing. I stood to speak and laughed as I told them, "Well, men, there's a first time for everything. If you told me six months ago I'd be standing in prison speaking to a seminary class of prisoners, I wouldn't have believed you. But, I bet that day you sat in the courtroom facing the judge as he read your sentence, you never thought you'd be here either." Heads nodded all over the room.

We weren't so different, them and me. God was blazing new territory for us both. As I spoke I realized God had forgiven their murders the same as he had forgiven me for losing my cool with my kids. The moment was surreal. We all sin, and the outcome is the same. For the wages of sin is death, but the gift of God is eternal life in Christ Jesus our Lord. (Romans 6:23 NIV)

I walked out of the prison that day speechless. God changes lives. He changed the lives of each of those men, and He changed mine. I left knowing His Word still holds true for us today. He does intend for us to feed the hungry, clothe the naked, nurse the sick, and visit those in prison. I'm not a missionary, or a chaplain, or even an ordained minister of any kind. So why did an ordinary mom go into the prison that day? Because I do believe we can change the world one person at a time. Only that day, I was the one changed.

Author: Carol Hatcher

Carol Hatcher is a Jesus lovin', coffee drinkin', boot wearin', sassy talkin' mother, speaker, and author - determined to live out Matthew 25:40 as an everyday missionary.

Sheeptotheright.com

Sugar Bowl Wisdom

While cleaning my kitchen just before Christmas, I noticed that the sugar bowl needed filling. No one in our house uses sugar-by-the-spoonful for anything, so it sat empty for months. Since the container was made of glass, I imagined it would look nicer if it was filled with what it was intended for. Thankfully, I found my bag of sugar without too much hunting and filled the jar. That task done, I finished my work in the kitchen and didn't give it a second thought.

Christmas Day arrived, precipitating snowy and white, and bringing with it treacherous roads for traveling. I was thankful we didn't have plans to be anywhere except home by the fire. As I glanced out the window just before lunchtime, I noticed a car pulled over to the side of the road. At first I saw no one, but soon a young woman emerged from the vehicle, walked around it, then got back in. Busy with my own family's holiday, I secretly hoped maybe she just stopped to make a phone call or enjoy the snowy scenery. But when she got out of her car the second time, her eyes met mine and I saw distress.

I called for my husband, who quickly dressed for the weather and headed out the side door. "Come on in," I called to her from the window, knowing she would want relief from the sleet and snow that was falling heavily. As I welcomed in this stranger, I could see she was shaken, her clothes wet and cold from the weather, her nerves shattered. "I just didn't want to hit the trees," she said, "so I headed for the ditch on the side of the road." She told me her name was Liz, and that she was headed to work just a few more miles away. "I'm not driving any more today though, " she declared as she called a friend to come pick her up.

After all the proper calls and arrangements had been made I realized we had plenty of time on our hands before anyone would be arriving to help her. What does one do with a complete stranger in their house on Christmas Day? Still noticing her damp clothes and trembling hands, I offered her a cup of tea. She readily accepted, and as it was brewing we chatted about where she grew up, where she attended school, and her love of her profession- hotel management.

When the tea was ready, I asked, "Would you like sugar or milk?" She said sugar was fine, and I reached for the recently stocked canister, thinking to myself how convenient it was that I had filled it just the other day, and now I didn't have to make Liz wait while I went scrambling through cupboards looking for a five-pound bag to serve from.

As she was putting the sugar into her mug, something quietly shifted in her mood, and she looked down wistfully at her spoon as it stirred the sweetener into the dark liquid. She started to speak, and I heard the choked-up emotion come through in her voice. Keeping her misty eyes on her tea, she said slowly, "My grandfather used to say, 'Always keep your sugar bowl filled, because you never know when you're going to have company' and 'It's the sweet things in life you'll remember'. If I ever own a hotel of my own someday, I'm going to name it The Sugar Bowl, after him."

I stared blankly. I'm sure I looked composed on the outside, but on the inside my proverbial jaw was wide open in amazement as I mentally connected my simple cleaning chore of filling an empty sugar bowl a week ago to this moment of witnessing the now-filled container having the power to evoke precious memories for a woman I had just met.

I thought back to how casually I had filled the container that day, more for looks than anything else. I couldn't have known that I would need it shortly thereafter in entertaining a stranded young gal on Christmas Day, whose grandfather's memory - along with his sugar bowl wisdom - obviously brought her close to tears. I saw God's hand in our visit and was filled with awe.

Time passed, my husband got her car out of the ditch, the police had their report, and her friend arrived to drive her the rest of the way to work. But before she left, we took the opportunity to tell her, "Liz, maybe it's more than coincidence that you got stuck outside our house on Christmas Day. Maybe God designed this to happen." We gave her a gospel tract and suggested that she read it at her leisure. She tucked it in her purse and assured us that she would. As she left, my husband and I prayed silently that God would use the whole amazing episode to bring her to Himself.

Stranger? Angel? A lost soul in need of a Savior? We can't say, but we know it impacted our family's Christmas. And if I ever happen to drive by an inn named The Sugar Bowl, I can be sure that it's owned and operated by a lovely gal named Liz who had a very wise grandfather, and whose car got providentially stuck in a ditch outside our home one cherished Christmas Day.

Author: Beth Coulton

I'm a writer, wife, sister, daughter and mom. I love laughter, chocolate and Jesus. May what's written here sweeten your heart as well as your day!

BethCoulton.com

A Gift From My Father

Photography was a semi-professional hobby of my Dad's, and he LOVED IT.

Late in his life, when I fortunate to know him as both a father and friend, I recall him heading out with his Nikon D-80 on a Saturday morning to just… "take pictures." After many years of shooting film and spending time in the downstairs lavette (a.k.a.his dark room), my Dad had finally embraced technology and was taking great pleasure in learning the nuances of composing, shooting, and editing digital pictures. He took some amazing shots and, because he still saw value in printing and framing them, we got to share in their beauty.

My Dad had a great eye…

My high school and college girlfriends will tell you that they never needed to worry about it, because "Jaime always had the camera." I enjoyed capturing the moments at special occasions and when gathering with people who were important to me. An eye for composition, a point-and-shoot camera, and the joy of sharing my pictures with others was about the extent of my connection to photography. I enjoyed it no doubt, but had no real ambition to take my "hobby" any further.

In January of 2010 my father suddenly passed away. In preparation for his memorial service I took responsibility for compiling photos of his life to share with others who had also loved him. It was one of the most emotionally difficult projects I have ever undertaken.

During the course of it I would discover three important things:

My father led a blessed life.

The love he gave during his life would undoubtedly live on.

Over the years, I had apparently taken a LOT of pictures.

We prepared to head back to Rhode Island after a period of grieving with my family. With tears in her eyes, my mother asked me to "Pick something." She wanted my brother and I to select something meaningful of my Dad's to have as our own.

From that day forward, I would be a faithful steward of my father's cameras and all that they captured.

In August of 2011, my dear friend, mentor and colleague, George L. Ortiz, Jr. started a grassroots ministry with his family. It was called The Elisha Project. As he recounted the events and emotions of a third consecutive Saturday spent feeding hand-made bagged lunches to the homeless, I felt undeniably drawn to support them. My Dad's Nikon D-80 appeared in my minds-eye and I knew that providing images which would allow us to share this project with others was exactly what God was calling me to do.

This summer The Elisha Project will celebrate their two-year anniversary. 90+ weeks of feeding people's stomachs and spirits, bringing families together in the act of selfless giving, and changing hearts. I am truly blessed to have captured and experienced many of those Saturdays. The photos, and the videos George created from them, have helped to draw over 29,000 people to follow the project on Facebook and hundreds of families to actively support and participate in it.

The spiritual journey prompted by my father's passing and the opportunity to be part of The Elisha Project opened my eyes, got me off the couch, and have changed my heart in ways that I never could have anticipated.

Today, I am pursuing my own photography business on a full-time basis… and am blessed to be sharing this precious gift from my Dad (and from my Heavenly Father) with the world.

Author: Jaime Lind

After many years in marketing, I met Christ and am now following His lead as I pursue my passion... using emotionally compelling photography to inspire and engage people in a unique and personal way.

IntegrityVenturesLLC.com

Flawed Potato Love

I had gotten the call. My pulse raced. Anxiety tore at my thoughts.

I knew life, from this point on, would be different. More different than I had ever imagined it would be.

I had been feeling for some time that life would soon change significantly. A proverbial "change in the wind." Well, there it was. Plain as day; the dramatic, dynamic difference I'd been praying for.

So I hopped on a plane. At the airport I talked with a man travelling to go see family. We talked about sports, about Tim Tebow (as it was during his great craze of 2011), and some other things I don't remember. I was too full of adrenaline to take in real conversation. After boarding, I sat between two very nice ladies who wanted to know everything about my family and my life and career.

This new life was going to be interesting, given the circumstances. I was only twenty-eight after all, and something like this doesn't normally happen to people my age. It was a very unique experience and I knew I ought to make special efforts to remember every moment, every feeling, every detail.

During a plane change, one of my best friends, who had airline employee privileges, met me at the gate, a special blessing that nobody gets to do these days under normal circumstances. He brought me food for the occasion. I thanked him and I tried to eat, but the butterflies in my stomach were too much and I was only able to take a few small bites. You know that feeling when you have either such fear or excitement that you just can't think of dulling it with carbohydrates? That was the feeling in the pit of my stomach, and it held true to its modus operandi.

My friend gave me some much needed encouragement and saw me off to my second plane, the one that would take me to my destination.

Where was my destination, you ask? Why, my new life of course! The one I'd prayed for, remember... That change in the wind that I'd so desperately desired.

My destination... was her.

My final plane landed, and I met my ride at the curb. I carried no luggage; the call had come so suddenly, I'd had no time to pack. On the way there, I rode in silence, again too full of anxiety to think of anything but the woman that waited at the end of my long journey.

I've known her most of my life, and we met when we were just children. You could say we grew up together in our own little world, with the common childlike experiences and misconceptions we shared together growing into a beautiful, unbreakable link that would last our entire life. She was breathtakingly gorgeous, energetic, uncompromisingly loyal, and carefree to a fault.

And I was going home to see her, my baby sister.

The breeze of air pressure blew my hair across my face as I walked through the sliding double doors, and walked to the back hallway to find the right room.

The pristine smell of anesthetic and hand sanitizer assailed my nostrils as I strode closer to the ICU.

There she lay, her face swollen from her head's impact with the windshield. Part of her skull had been removed to relieve the pressure on her brain. What hair they hadn't shaved off was matted with blood. She was intubated, and breathed only with the help of a machine.

Remember the part where I prayed for a change? Right.

Nine *very* short hours later, a mere twenty-one hours after my 3 a.m. phone call... the one nobody ever wants to receive... I said my last goodbyes to my twenty-three year-old little sister, Courtney Ann, on Thanksgiving, and my life would be different. Forever changed.

Talk about getting me off the couch.

I spoke at her memorial service. I spoke of sadness, grief and typical things. But most of all I spoke about hope. The hope that people only accept in the face of extreme hopelessness. The hope that everyone wants, but most ignore in favor of living life on a comfortable couch, and only embrace when they are faced with the prospect of the couch disintegrating beneath them.

Because my couch was gone.

Courtney was a person whom, despite her faults and vices (as everyone has), LOVED everyone she cared to know so fully and unabashedly. She brought life to her friends, instead of demanding life from them. I may have judged her for spending money frivolously, but she spent on others. She *invested*.

What had I been investing in? Impossible tasks like finding a perfect friend, writing the perfect song, or making a perfect marriage. While I may have been feeling hurt and slighted, I only cared about things within easy reach of my La-Z-Boy.

What changed me? It was the four-hundred plus people that showed up to celebrate the short time they had with a person that showed love. Flawed love, maybe, but she showed it. As if someone could ever love perfectly in this life... Courtney didn't invite people to her safe place; she visited them in theirs.

So, here I am today, trying to show more love. Flawed potato love...

And friends, might I remind you that it is *not* easy to love people. In fact, so many people who think they are "loving others" are really hurting them, either by enabling them or controlling them. Real love is discipline and honesty and pointing people to others who will love them, too.

Real love is getting people off their own couch and helping them kill their own potato-ish-ness.

Don't wait for your world to change to get off yours. Be a rebel, and get up.

Author: Marc Sandin

*Consumed as a child with perfection;
Spending the rest of life overcoming the
need for it. Continuing that dedication with
the words, thoughts, keyboard, pen, paper.
Encouraging others to have perspective and
joy and to love well.*

WriteRite.org

A Weary Mom, A Sacred Meal

It was so hot that day. Well over ninety degrees. The church had no air conditioning. I noticed you from the kitchen where I was preparing the meals to be passed out to the neighborhood children that came in for our VBS (Vacation Bible School). Each night this week, different small groups would prepare and serve a meal. That night happened to be my turn. All day I had prayed for VBS and the meal that would be served. I prayed for a break in the heat. I prayed for opportunity. To do what? I am not sure. But opportunity to do something that mattered. Something significant.

You had brought your own four children and a few from your neighborhood. You all had walked in the heat. You took care of all the kids making certain that they all behaved, used their manners, ate their meal and cleaned up the table. They then went on to participate with the other kids, leaving you to sit alone on the bench in the fellowship hall.

I asked you if you would like for me to box up some of the dinners to take home. You quickly said, "Yes, that would be helpful. Anything would help."

Shortly after, we noticed boxes of bread from Panera Bread that had been donated.

I walked across the fellowship hall again to ask you if you would like some bread and/or bagels. Again, you replied, "Anything would be helpful." When I gave you some choices, asking you what the children would enjoy, you sheepishly said, "They will eat what is put in front of them. It is better than not having anything at all."

I returned to the kitchen and wrapped up some breads and a variety of bagels and brought them over to you. You graciously took them and I returned to the kitchen to finish cleaning up.

As I went to leave for the night, you were still sitting on the bench. I approached you, hand extended and introduced myself and we shook hands. Your eyes filled with tears as you told me that it had been a long time since anyone had extended a hand to you. I stopped and we chatted for a bit.

Weary mother, you shared that you're a single mom. You're raising four children on your own. Your parents are older and you also take care of them. You shared that life has been lonely for you. I could see that you were worn and tired and feeling down. We continued sharing how exhausting children can be at times, and yet you stated that you wouldn't change a thing.

Lord, how can our eyes be closed to the captives that weep while no one sees? How do we drive to church and not realize that every single door represents a story? A story of a life... a life that has struggles and pain that no one notices.

And then you said something that pierced me. I will never forget. Not ever.

"I haven't smiled in a long time. But you made me smile tonight. Thank you."

My eyes filled with tears, and you continued....

"I haven't been to church in a long time either. Maybe I should try coming. What time is church here?"

"10:30."

You asked, "Do I need to be dressed up to come?".

Never have I been so happy to honestly reply. "See what I am wearing now? This is what I wore on Sunday." I motioned to my clothes.

I don't know many that I would have admitted that to so freely but somehow I was pleased as punch to tell you. Same clothes.

And you replied, "Amen, sister! Now that I *can* do. Wear the same clothes on Sunday and then again in a few days. This may be the church for me!"

We talked a few minutes more. I left to drive home. Sobered and tearful. The entire ride.

"And if you give even a cup of cold water to one of the least of my followers, you will surely be rewarded." (Matthew 10:42 NLT)

Lord, what about chicken nuggets, some tater tots, carrot sticks and watermelon?

Weary Mom, never has a meal seemed so sacred. Weary Mom, thank you for reminding me this week that there truly is great reward and blessing in the small things. For surely, it was I that received that night.

Author: Joanne Viola

Wife, mom, Mimi that loves God, finds joy in life and just wants to share Him with others.

Daysnthoughts.com

Wells in Africa: My Dream

It was the happiest night of my life. Here I was at twelve years old, dancing with tribe members on the other side of the world. The drumbeats pounded in my chest. I felt the Lord's presence like I've never felt before while I danced in a circle with my new Ghanaian friends. Together, we were dancing for Jesus while bugs the size of Oreos buzzed all around us. But that didn't stop us from dancing.

This crazy adventure started a year before when my parents talked about the need for wells and water in Africa around the dinner table. When I started sixth grade, I decided to run for treasurer of my school. I had to write a speech and wanted to have something catchy in my speech. So I decided to use raising money to dig wells in Africa as my main point. Unfortunately, I lost the election.

I came home from school very sad. I told my mom what happened, and she thought I was sad because I lost the election. I stopped her and said, "Mom, it's not that. Now I can't raise money for wells in Africa. God has burned in my heart a desire to dig wells in Africa and I can't get that out of my heart."

That night my parents were having dinner with our missions pastor. He decided to open an account at church so I could raise money for wells on my own. Right after that I had to decide which country in Africa I would help. Our church had well projects in two places: Nigeria and Ghana. I prayed about the decision and I chose Ghana.

Soon I found out that there was a village in Northern Ghana called Sankpem that desperately needed water. Almost every year, a woman died trying to get water for her family. I found out there was a team of people going to the same area of Ghana in the summer. So my mom and I raised money to go to Ghana with the team. And I also raised money to complete the well project in Sankpem.

While we were waiting to go I got two discouraging emails about the well project. The well-digging company drilled once, but did not hit water. They tried again, and still didn't hit water. Despite all that, I still wanted to visit Sankpem for myself.

In June of 2008, we flew to Ghana. We started out in a town in Northern Ghana called Tamale. Every day I went out with my translator, Emmanuel, into the slums near a seminary and shared about Jesus with the people. I told them the story about God creating the world all the way through to Jesus' death and resurrection. I got to see a lot of Muslims come to faith in Jesus. Before I went to Ghana I prayed one person would meet Jesus. And here I was seeing several people come to Him.

Later during the trip I got to see Sankpem. About 1,000 people live in Sankpem, and about twenty adults attend church there. I saw little children playing in the fields, and I watched as a lady walked past us, a huge jar of water on her head. I stood on the two places where they tried to dig wells. The ground was all dry rock, no water. The village elder told us, "We're very sorry that you spent all that money and we still didn't get water. If we had hit water, we'd be having celebrations right now." We prayed that one day Sankpem would have water in their village.

I hope that a pipeline can be made from Sankpem's nearest village neighbor about ten kilometers away. I'm raising money for that (cost approximately $10,000) and for a rainwater capturing system for the village. Next year, when I go to Sankpem, I pray the village elder will be holding a huge celebration because water has come to Sankpem.

This trip has changed me in many ways. I don't take the water that comes out of my faucet at home for granted. I'm not as much of a consumer as I used to be. I now have many friends on the other side of the world that taught me how to truly follow Jesus and trust Him for everything. One of my friends said that for ten years he never knew when his next meal was coming, but he learned to trust God. I want to have that kind of faith in God, not in stuff.

I never knew that at the beginning of my sixth grade year that God would take me from a failed election to where I am now. Losing the election was probably the best thing that happened in my life. I will never be the same.

What I'd love to see is a bunch of young people like myself to begin to dream bigger dreams, dreams that only God can give, dreams that only He can bring about. My dream is to bring water to a village on the other side of the world. What is your dream?

Author: Aidan DeMuth

Aidan DeMuth is a high school student who loves to travel and had an adventure of raising funds for an African well when he was in the sixth grade.

Five Parents and One Set of Twins

He says we pick him up too late.
He needs a cell phone - so he can text his big brother.
He expels far too much gas from his body.
He's my third child. 13.

She speaks more words than 10 humans combined.
She loves organizing her room - keeping track.
She takes three or more photos of life - every day.
She's my second born. 15.

He's off to work at Chick-fil-A - so handsome in his uniform.
He's got his first girlfriend. His first car.
He'll be the first to leave in two short years.
He's my first practice as a mom. 16.

Mother of three teenagers. Most would cringe.

I delight, even when the day is devastating, they are mine. They
let me in. We hold hope together.

Davis, 13, came home a few weeks ago from school. He was so
wrecked with the flu, crying up the staircase, heaving sobs, so
worn out. I watched him sleep that day. Wishing I could take the
pain instead.

I want to be just like Davis when I grow up. He wears long socks,
gym shorts, and a polo to school. He is free.
Free from caring what "they" think.
Free being exactly him, and joyfully mine.

Kylie, 15, told us this year about her depression. She hid her very rough year from us. Maybe we should have seen the isolation. Maybe we should have heard her cries for help. But she shared it. Finally. Soon enough for us to fight hard with her.

When your child tells you they want to harm themselves, there's nothing more cutting. Her young life will understand when others are broken. Her heart will serve them well.

Wil, 16, so open about his faith, deeply desires that others would live in the freedom that he is finding every day. He quietly displays humility and power, all wrapped into one. What kid has a 60 year old mentor? What kid calls others to live for more - on his Facebook? What kid? Wil does.

They didn't choose adoption. We asked them about it. But we chose it.

They were 8, 11, and 12 when our 3 year-old foster twins came.

Young.
Tender.
Innocent.

We'd prepared them as best we could - like preparing a toddler to fight a tiger - like David setting up to battle Goliath.

Prepared?
Ready?
Equipped?

Not ever.

Willing?

Open?
Trusting in the God Who Can?

Absolutely!

Without our three older kids on board, there are days we wonder, as the adoptive parents - would we have made it through the "twins" without having our older kids loving alongside us?

Surely God would have given help in some other way. But he chose our birth children to serve our adopted children. He chose to bless two wounded, lonely, hurting 3 year-olds with five parents.

Five hearts giving.
Five faces smiling.
Five hope givers - loving two hopeless kids.

Our little ones wandered around those first few months, blindsided, confused, seeking survival and defense.

Our big kids watched in wonder - this is real? We get to love these two little strangers?

We didn't know what foods they liked.
We didn't know what they could and couldn't do.
We didn't know much.

But we knew this:
We loved.
Because He first loved.
Us.

We gave.
Because He gave us.
Hope.

We prayed.
Because what else could we do?
Believing.

Gloria wouldn't learn Kylie's name. She referred to her as "that girl".
Dalton followed his older twin around, hiding, barely speaking for months.

Three and a half. We'd have thought potty trained, sleeping through the night. Some maturities mastered?

Not so much.

They both called us "Mom" and "Dad" immediately.
We were obvious choices, since the other three called us by these names.

That first year of foster care was a blur. I know we all grew up that year - more than any other year before - or after.

It's still hard some days.
Some. Many. They're all kinds of days mixed into one lifetime of family.

My teenagers hold me accountable.
"Mom, you're being a little hard on him."
"Mom, she didn't mean to do that."

My little ones build my character - and increase my need for Christ's strength.

"Mommy, I gave my $20 to a kid on the bus." ($20 for a library fine - not simply for a strange kid on bus).

"Mommy, I screamed at my Sunday school teacher today. I didn't want to do the lesson."

My husband and I... we wait.
Patiently.

My husband and I - the two grown up parents -with three co-parents - and one set of 8 year-old twins - we love.
Severely.
Without reserve.
Without return.

Because love doesn't waste a single minute.
Because when love is easy, it isn't really love at all.

Author: Jenny Price

Pastor's wife. I like my husband. Mom to five. I love teenagers. My twins mold my heart. Blogger. Coach. Mentor. Friend. I bleed hope. I hold onto what I profess in Christ - and help you do the same.

iwokeupyesterday.com

A Beautiful Disruption

"Don't give up hope."

The words came from my son's pediatrician a few weeks after my 7-month-old had been hospitalized for Infantile Spasm Syndrome (ISS), a rare form of childhood epilepsy.

Born in December, Josiah, our first child, began exhibiting some unusual symptoms in early July. He was lethargic, would drop his head suddenly during feedings, and rolled his eyes to the top of his head several times a day.

I called the pediatrician and was told that babies do a variety of "new" things at this age and that I shouldn't be too concerned. But by the third week of July, he was stiffening his limbs while rolling his eyes and we were convinced he was having seizures. We took him to the emergency room on a Saturday morning.

Rewind three years. I'd met my husband, Kevin, just when I was feeling as if I'd be single forever. I'd recently turned 30 and met my husband when he made my latte at Starbucks. It's ironic that we met over one of my more superficial passions-good coffee-when we actually shared a deeper life passion-children. He was going to be a children's pastor. I'd been involved in children's ministry most of my life. It was a match made in heaven.

A little over a year after we met, Kevin and I married, and six months after that we learned we were pregnant with our first child. My six-hour labor and delivery went off without a hitch. God had fulfilled many of my dreams in a short space of time and seemingly ushered me into idyllic family life.

But seven short months into motherhood, I realized something was wrong with my baby. Infantile Spasm is just rare enough that many pediatricians have never seen a case of it, which is why ours didn't catch it. But when Josiah was diagnosed by a neurologist at the hospital, we learned that catching ISS at its onset is crucial to treatment and recovery. Even then, treating ISS can be tricky and a percentage of children don't respond.

Our first night in the hospital, I looked up Infantile Spasm on the Internet. What I read was terrifying. I learned that uncontrolled, ISS causes mental retardation. By the time spasms fade away on their own around 2 or 4 years old, it is too late for the child to regain the development that has been lost. In some worst-case scenarios I found on forums, parents were caring for teenagers who had only developed to a 3-month level.

Just a month earlier, Josiah had been a happy, active infant, passing his 6-month check-up with flying colors. But by the time he left the hospital, he had the motor skills of a baby half his age. I was terrified. We started him on high doses of steroids - the treatment with the best prognosis. If it worked, it was possible Josiah would have a full developmental recovery.

I prayed we hadn't caught it too late. What if it doesn't work? The question shot fear through my entire being. Both Kevin and I struggled with the sadness of what was happening to our baby.

The seizures stopped, but Josiah seemed to regress even more as the steroids took their toll. An EEG a week after we left the hospital showed that the electrical charges in his brain were still abnormal - not what the neurologist had hoped for.

"We'll just have to wait and see," he said.

A week later, I sat in the pediatrician's office, worst-case scenarios consuming my mind.

"Don't give up hope," she said, touching my arm gently.

I felt foolish that someone I barely knew had to tell me this, but I knew her message came straight from my heavenly Father who loved me and cared for Josiah.

From that point on, I began meditating on the truths God offered me in His Word: "Josiah is fearfully and wonderfully made;" "I have a plan for him;" "I love the little children." These simple truths reminded me that God was at work, even when I couldn't see what He was doing.

During those days, I had to trust in God's care many times when I couldn't see evidence of healing. As Josiah's little body puffed up from the steroids, making him look like a sumo wrestler, I held onto God's promise that He was an ever-present help.

The Lord faithfully encouraged Kevin and me during that time. One evening, after church, we went to one of our favorite restaurants even though we knew it wasn't wise with hospital bills stacking up. After the meal (a shared appetizer and entrée), the server approached us and said someone had paid for our meal. We looked around but recognized no one.

God was so tender in those days. He generously gave us the grace and strength we needed through the kindnesses of others and the comfort of His own presence.

And slowly things began to get better.

Once Josiah was off the steroids, his high blood pressure and other symptoms lessened. He relearned to roll over, then sit up, then crawl. Finally, just before his second birthday, our little boy learned to walk.

Josiah is now a happy 28-month-old who loves giving kisses and bursts out in a hearty, "Ha, HA!" many times a day. He remains developmentally delayed but continues to catch up. He has been diagnosed with ataxia-an unbalanced gait when walking-caused by his seizures.

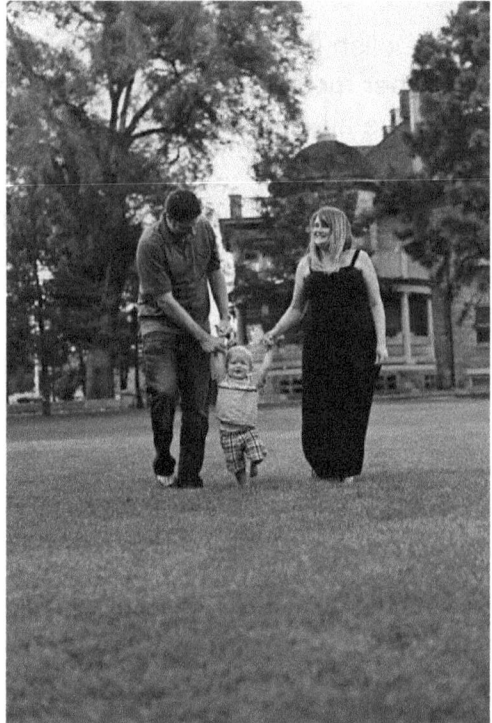

We don't know the extent of what we will face with Josiah and possible disabilities. We do know that God has given us an extraordinary little boy who makes our lives better.

Josiah's name means "Jehovah heals." Because of him, I've seen a side of my faithful Father I would not have known apart from this tragic disruption of my dreams. God did not give me a "normal" first-time mom experience, but He has used my son to show me the depths of His love and care for me.

Author: Suzanne Gosselin

*Suzanne Hadley Gosselin is a freelance
writer and editor who has written for Focus
on the Family, Zondervan, and David C.
Cook. She enjoys coffee, and spending time
with her family.*

BoundlessLine.org

Earthquake Moments

Clouds flew by and the engine rumbled as we made our descent. Stepping out onto the tarmac in humid sticky air, I stared in disbelief at the tent of an airport in front of me. Culture shock continued to set in as we drove through the streets. United Nation workers were on the streets. Tents stood where homes used to. People flooded the trash dump looking for what they could find, as fires roared around them.

We were no longer in New England with cool weather and large houses. We were in Haiti.

A poor country to begin with, the earthquake had knocked them down even further. The earthquake had destroyed their homes, had devastated their food, and had caused instability with their electricity. But the earthquake had not destroyed their resolve or spirit, it had made it stronger.

Through the day we helped rebuild a Church and school that was destroyed. Cement bucket by cement bucket we filled the pillars and saw the second story, their sanctuary, come together as school students learned below. Recess saw hundreds of students piled in the dirt below us, smiling as they saw their building, their school, continue to be built. We looked out through the windows at the UNICEF tent that was the current sanctuary and served as the classrooms for the preschool. These students were learning and growing but they couldn't wait to be settled.

Our afternoons were filled with orphanages. Kids separated from their parents, some by death and some by choice, clung to us for comfort, affection, and love. The balloon animals I made, although received with happy faces, didn't seem like enough.

One of the house mom's stood on our bus as we were about to leave with tears in her eyes. She spoke of the earthquake, how devastating it had been for their country, for her people. And she spoke of the future. This woman in front of us spoke of how that earthquake had changed her country for the better. She looked at this tragedy as a blessing from God, an answer to their prayers. Now people knew that Haiti existed. People groups, charities, organizations were flocking to Haiti to help. God was sending His people to come and bring money, supplies, and labor that were so desperately needed. And none of it would have happened without the earthquake.

It's true you know. I didn't really know much about Haiti until the earthquake. I didn't know that it was a country that was poverty stricken, had beautiful scenery, and even more amazing people. And I never would have gone, or spoken in the school's chapel, or made balloon animals, or held orphans, or poured cement buckets to build a church if it hadn't been for the earthquake.

When we came back home, I realized that our life and this world are filled with earthquake moments. Moments of destruction and devastation that are actually the answer to our many prayers. Through those moments, God opens the door for help, blessing, and restoration; for people to move and be used by Him to do great things.

What is your earthquake moment? What destruction or devastation lies before you that God can use to open the door to your blessing? Seize the moment, get off the couch, take the step, and go through the open door. The blessing and answered prayer may just exist through that moment.

Author: Danielle Christy

Writer, youth pastor's wife, and mom of 2 kids. Trying my best to live life to the fullest in ministry, with kids, and with Jesus.

Christyswithkids.blogspot.com

Sarah's Song

Icy cold gripped downtown Billings Montana in it's talons. There was nothing surprising in that, at this time of year a blanket of snow and frigid air often clung to the city's skin. Despite the cold my husband and I had found our way to the local Wal-Mart during a break from the pastor's conference we were attending.

Pulling up to a stop sign headed out of the parking lot I saw her. She was crouched in the snow, white hair sticking out from under a stocking cap, bleary blue eyes telling the story of hardship. Those eyes locked on mine and it was too late, I felt their grip in the pit of my stomach.

"Let me out," I said to my husband. Wordlessly he unlocked the car door and I jumped out as he went through the stop sign and drove in a circle to park in a nearby parking spot.

I approached her and knelt to her level. "Do you have a place to stay?" I asked.

"A tent," she pointed, "I stay in a tent back there." There was a flash of spirit in her eyes, a tenacity of life.

"In this weather," I asked. "Is there not somewhere else you can stay?"

"The shelter only keeps men, they don't have a place for women." And she launched into an explanation peppered with names and details I had no reference for.

"Well, is there anything I can get you? What do you need?"

She wanted coffee and long johns, maybe a scarf. "I'll be back." I grabbed her hands, squeezed them, and we smiled at each other.

Back in Walmart I chose a pair of long underwear, a soft, cream colored scarf, and gloves. From the gas station nearby a large coffee, and if I recall, some food.

I brought the plastic bags, like an offering, back to where she was huddled in the cold. Glad to help it still felt trite in the face of such need.

She was delighted and thankful though. As she spoke, slurring over her gap toothed smile, I pieced together a life of predictable tragedy. She said her name was Sarah; such a pretty name in the face of harshness. Addiction, hard times, lost children that were still grieved and missed, it was a story of struggle.

I listened and nodded. Then compelled, and surprising even myself, I clasped her hands and said, "Sarah, do you know Jesus?"

Her weathered face beamed, "Oh yes, I know Jesus." And we talked about the Savior who comforted her even in this place of suffering. I prayed with her and wished her well.

As I turned to go she stopped me. "Can I sing you a song?"

I smiled. "Of course you can." Kneeling back down to her level I braced myself to endure some horrible caterwaul.

But I was wrong. As we squatted there on the corner, in the snow, with cars passing by, I was taught a lesson about beauty.

Rising up from the inside of Sarah came a love song, sung rich and mellow. It poured out and washed my feet even as I had sought to wash hers. I wish I could remember the name of it now. It was a country song that talked about Jesus' love, but more important than the song was how it was sung. With conviction and fervor.

As the last notes died away tears glistened in our eyes. I stood quietly, what more could be said, and left her in the snow. Turning back, I waved. She smiled.

I got into my warm car and drove away, silent. We went back to the pastor's conference. I don't remember the message, but it couldn't have been more powerful than the one I had just received. For a moment, in Billings Montana, in the snow, on a corner outside of Walmart, I had stood on holy ground.

Author: Beck Gambill

Following Jesus all the way home. I write about the journey, people that inspire, and beauty all around. I'm looking for mercy at every turn.

BeckGambill.wordpress.com

The Letter

You don't know this yet, but you're the best part of my life. I've dreamed of you for so long it's almost as if I painted you to life. Those soft blue eyes, the sandy brown hair, and the giggle that sends me to the happiest of places.

I've been waiting to say those two little words out loud. To scream it to the world that you, my dream, are here. Those words that so many have been able to say before.

"I'm pregnant."

But with each passing day, the words don't come. I know you're just waiting for the perfect moment to surprise me. You're clever that way, just like me.

It seems like ages ago I was diagnosed with Endometriosis. That was a strange and sad day for me. I didn't understand what that meant at first but now that I do, I think that when you finally do want to make your first appearance, I'll be happier than most. We will have beat the odds and for us, that's a miracle. But for now, I'm teetering on the the edge between tragedy and a blessing. With my diagnosis, the odds are against us but that won't bring me down just yet. The doctors have hope but I think they hold out hope so that I find the light somewhere. So that I have something to hang on to. I hear stories of happy endings but also hear about others who accepted the fact that they would never be mothers. But I am a mother. I am your mother.

When I see all the other mommies with their round bellies waiting for their babies to arrive it's almost automatic that I place my own hand on my own belly, almost willing you to be there. But you're still not. It breaks my heart because I have wanted nothing more than to have you, and years have gone by.

The doctors tell me that there are many ways to force you into my world but I want you to know that I would prefer you to come when you're ready. But, I can only wait so long, my sweet dream. Time is not on my side like it is on yours, I'm afraid. If you wait too long then I will never get to feel the soft wrinkles behind your neck. Or run my finger over the tiny indents where your knuckles will soon be. I would give up everything just to rock you to sleep at night.

The journey the doctors suggest is a long and trying one. It's not going to be easy for me but I think you're worth every obstacle. The decision to go to the fertility clinic was an easy one. But as time goes on, I feel the struggle with my emotions beginning. I'm worried that after all the efforts, you still won't come. Is it possible? Possible that I will never hear your heartbeat? That I will never get to feel the "bond" that all the mothers talk about constantly? Will I miss out on painted pictures and report cards on the refrigerator? Is it possible?

I suppose it's not impossible but I refuse to allow these thoughts the merit they want. I want you to know that I am your mother. Whether you come in this lifetime or not, you're the greatest thing to happen to me. The greatest dream I ever held on to. And I will hold on.

So when it comes time that the doctors help you along, just know that it is because I couldn't wait any longer to see you. I promise that after I tell the world my two worded news, I will let you make your own decisions, within reason, regarding your timeliness. Infertility is a word I do not allow a definition. I do believe, however, that the doctors will find a way for us to be together and oh what an adventure it will be! The journey I'm about to embark on is a scary one and probably at times one that will leave me feeling completely alone and on my knees begging. If it wasn't for you, this dream I have, I wouldn't be going forward with this. I wouldn't do a thing about it. Not to mention, I'm doing it in a hospital that speaks your father's language. But you, my dream, are worth it.

In my mind, you're the greatest human who has not yet begun to live and there is so much world and incredible experiences I want to share with you. Lucky for you, you will grow up bilingual. You are going to be a child who knows things. Who has opinions and understands culture. A child who soaks up languages and accepts others for their own beliefs. I have no doubt that after all the journeys I've been on and all the things I've learned, you will find a way to teach me more.

You are the reason for my adventure in this new world of medicine. You will be the goal and I keep looking forward to that moment that our eyes meet. I'll know right then that it was all worth it. And because of that, I am not afraid.

Author: Kaitlin Clark

Blog writer, dog lover, wine drinker, obsessed with martinis, pumpkin, and peanut butter (creamy). All American-Irish girl living in Germany with her German love and adapting to this crazy culture!

TheDiaryofSugarandSpice.wordpress.com

Polio: Vaccinating a Nation

I hardly knew what polio was before I ventured into Indian territory. You vaguely hear about it abroad; part of the routine vaccination program for children but never spoken about further. The first instance that slapped me in the face is the picture of my eight year old student, Ramesh, running through the dusty playground yelling 'didi' 'didi!' (a respectful term for Aunt/ teacher in Hindi) as I walked through the school gate, reminding me that I had left something behind in the classroom. He was gripping his leg with his hand, wobbling, smiling in fact, big white teeth beaming, impressed that he had reminded me that I had forgotten my bag of stencils. He limped back to the classroom. The classroom has no pens, no paper, no color, no desks or chairs. There was Ramesh struggling to sing and dance, pushed around by the other kids due to his disability.

I had always wanted to teach English abroad. I had always wanted to travel to India. I had never envisaged that I would be learning the Hindi words for 'be quiet', 'make a circle,' 'make a line' and 'all together now' let alone be teaching third grade mathematics and English in a rural community named Bedla 10 km from Udaipur in India's northern state of Rajasthan. So here I am. And two weeks into my teaching it is polio vaccination week.

We wake up early on Saturday morning to visit the local hospital and prepare for vaccination day. The van bumps along the dirt streets of Bedla. A 'village' in Indian terms, a 'city' in Australian terms.

After ten minutes we arrive at the dilapidated local hospital. We creep up the concrete stairs, trying to avoid two vicious stray dogs. We enter. It is a very small hospital with no more than twenty rooms and beds. Some beds are in the hallway, medical equipment hanging precariously from the walls, trays and medical containers lye unsealed. Undefinable blotches on bed sheets: I turn my head. We walk into the Head Nurse's office. It is large with one small desk at the far corner. There is paper everywhere, two UNICEF fridges full of vaccinations, a few dingy looking chairs and small freezer boxes with stickers all over them from previous polio campaigns. 'Namaste' we greet her enthusiastically. We bow our heads in unison, she smiles warmly, her teeth glisten against her bright orange sari. She gives instructions in Hindi to Gaurav and Ravi, the two hard working volunteer coordinators.

First, we place pre-written Hindi stickers on each box. The stickers contain information about the village location and number of children to be vaccinated in each village. The data is gathered from the local daycare centers by teachers. No official data exists yet the system works flawlessly. We label about one hundred boxes. After a couple of hours we return home to fresh ginger chai.

The following day is the official polio vaccination day: February 25, 2013. Millions of community booths are set up around India, manned by hard working local volunteers. We hang a brightly colored poster on our van as a reminder for parents.

We are first asked to deliver vaccination vials and ice to community booths that run short. We drive through beautiful mountains and rural communities, everyone waving joyfully at us as we pass. We get offered some delicious lemongrass tea at one stop. The booth is outside the local day care center in the middle of a farming district. A few cows roam the dusty streets and suddenly a bright colored sari appears through the dust, nursing small children in arms. Women cover their faces with their saris, approaching shyly. Some children are exuberant, some are scared, others are shy, but one thing is for sure: every single Indian seems to know what polio is and are very receptive to their children being vaccinated.

The following two days we walk through small rural communities. We leave early in the van and pick up more supplies from the local hospital. We also pick up two extraordinary helpers: a local school teacher Mr. Dinesh, in his crisp white suit, and Indra, the village day care worker, wearing a beautiful golden sari and clinking jewellery around her ankles.

I follow Mr Dinesh's fast pace, in his crisp white clothing, marking each house with a 'P', a number, the date, and an arrow pointing a particular way: all method in the systematic process. I write with chalk on doors, windows, fences and walls of each house in the village. We travel from door to door, through sugar cane fields, through wheat fields, and over rock makeshift fences (even Indra in her sari!) We are greeted warmly by every single family.

We have one vial left. Ravi speaks with Mr. Dinesh who knows the community well. He points to the top of a steep hill. We literally hike up the mountain, grasping carefully onto our vaccination box. We arrive at a very small house made of mud. It has one room, a few clothes hanging from the hay covered roof and two goats outside. There is no door. We poke our head inside. A mother is holding her newborn child in her arms. 'Namaste' she says warmly, beckoning us to enter. Gaurav takes the final vial, places one, and then two drops into the small child's mouth. They all smile as we depart and the little family wave as we descend down the steep mountain. There is nothing around. No shops, no houses, no water supply, no electricity: Just a small family with a few goats in a mud house on top of a hill in rural India. And somehow they knew exactly why we were there.

Author: Ingrid Jansons

I am interesting, inspiring, and adventurous! I've prayed with monks in the Himalayas, I've lived in a Nepalese orphanage, I've backpacked my way through Siberia, and I've slept in an Norwegian igloo.

IngridJansons.wordpress.com

Never Alone

I wasn't standing there long before the corridor began to fill up with people. We adjusted the name tags around our necks, and didn't seem to mind being pressed together as we anticipated the doors opening soon. A worker with a megaphone at the front of the line was the only thing that was separating the crowd from the stairway that lead to the convention center. He spoke through a megaphone that barely carried over the buzz of the room. It seemed like he was apologizing for the wait, but for some, they had been waiting for this day for what seemed like forever. Some traveled miles to get here. Some traveled days. They didn't mind a few more minutes. For me, I couldn't help but look around and realize that I wasn't alone.

Because for me, the story of this gathering started some twenty years previously in a small classroom in a church building in a rural suburb of eastern Michigan. As a pre-college teen, I had been invited to attend a conference about, what would now be labeled, social justice. Caring for others that are disadvantaged. Overlooked. Some 300 of us were attending to know how we could best love our neighbor, and I happened to pick a topic from the list that was going to plant a seed within me that a young teenager couldn't have expected. That topic was Caring for the AIDS Community.

The man who led the session spoke with passion. He told stories of people he knew who were left alone, abandoned by their friends and family to die with this disease. At the time in the late 80s, little was known, but what was known was causing a lot of fear. A lot of inaction. A lot of judgment by those who were different. With pictures and statistics written on his overhead projector, his desire was to motivate us to care about those who were being afflicted by this mysterious illness that had no cure.

His plea to care was filled with a sense of urgency that I hadn't experienced before. Yet, looking around the room, I realized no one else knew its urgency. I couldn't help but notice that I was alone.

Of the 300 in the conference, less than 10 chose this session. The cold and empty brown folding chairs around me reverberated his facts and stories to ears that weren't there to hear them. The room felt empty. I felt like I was being given a charge that the world needed to hear, and I was the only one listening.

Why aren't more people here?
Why am I in here?
What could I possibly do to help?

I went off to college, wondering what this meant. How I could live with what I know and not act, even though it seemed like no one around me was interested or seemed to care.

The women gathered under the shade of an acacia tree in the middle of the northern Kenya desert village. The handwriting in black ink on the wooden door on the brick building next to them was labeled "Duran Dema HIV Support Group," a program supported by the organization I work for. It didn't take long after hearing their stories to understand why the group existed – why 'support' was necessary. They all had contracted HIV. They had all been disowned by their families, kicked out of their homes from husbands that had, more than likely, given them the disease in the first place. Modern day lepers. Alone.

Then they met Kabale. Kabale knew what it meant to have this disease. She also knew what it meant to feel the fear to share her status. And what it meant to feel alone. With courage, she started this group so no one ever had to feel alone like she did. She pleaded for a clinic to be built in the community so people didn't have to travel days for health care like she did. And her pleas were heard.

As the women shared their stories, I could look into their eyes and see the pain of the memories that brought them together in the first place. Yet, the bond they had was strong. They talked about their disease differently. They called it 'living positively' – almost as if it was a badge of purpose. A calling to live differently. A challenge to look beyond a status or a label.

In that community, I heard how the women were helping one another - ensuring they were going to the clinic, eating healthy, finding ways to earn a living. Support defined. They weren't alone anymore.

Standing in the packed hallway of the International AIDS Conference at the Convention Center in Washington DC, I wonder how many of the other people in the room felt the way I did the first time they learned of the disease. Whether they learned about it from a concert or basketball player or from a doctor telling them their own status, I wondered where their

185

journey to care began. For the tens of thousands gathered there, it was enough care to motivate them to come together under one cause.

As I walked past rows of booths of organizations from all over the globe sharing how they are impacting their community to urgently stop the spread of the disease or bringing a healthy, long life to those who are affected, my eyes filled with tears. It was at that moment that I realized that I wasn't alone. Maybe I was never alone. I thought of Kabale and the women under the acacia tree. Although we were in different communities, in different regions of the world, talking about HIV in different ways to different audiences, we were all together, we were the same.

Author: Mike Lenda

Engagement Director for Blood:Water Mission. Husband to a superhero, Daddy to 4 girls, Friend, Coffee Snob, Brand Loyalist, Aspiring Localvore, Lover of Laughter, Truth Seeker.

A Day with Dengue

I kept holding the trash can long after I'd finished throwing up, staring into it, thinking about nothing and everything all at once.

"You know this means we're taking you back to the hospital," said Kate Wilson, our resident nursing student.

I nodded silently, too worn out to speak, not sure whether to feel disappointed or relieved. It was the second time I'd thrown up in the space of a few hours, which meant my body hadn't retained any fluids since early that morning. Most people who die of dengue fever die from dehydration, and my college friends weren't about to let me get away with that.

Within ten minutes, there were four of us in Robbie Miller's car: Robbie driving, Kate navigating, Lydia Shewan offering me water at regular intervals, and me, clutching a makeshift barf bag and feeling the world lurch around me.

Then we were at Strong Hospital's Emergency Department-my second time there in three days. They put me in a wheelchair, gave me a bracelet with a barcode, and told us to wait. We found seats together too close to the front door, and I shivered every time someone came in or went out and let in a gust of January air.

The television kept advertising overpriced underclothes and websites for Christian singles. I had seen the same commercials before, but today I watched them with a new pair of eyes. Played on the plasma screen of that Emergency Department waiting room, they became shallow, vapid, unimportant. I didn't want more nifty kitchen appliances or a boost for my love life. Today, all I wanted was another year, another week, another hour to begin doing all the things I'd put off for later.

Funny how brushing up against death can teach us so much about coming alive.

Every time one of my friends looked over to see how I was doing, I would grin back, just so they knew I was still me. I could feel myself turning grey. I recited Philippians 4 under my breath: "Rejoice in the Lord always… The Lord is near… Do not be anxious about anything… The peace of God, which transcends all understanding…"

Across from us sat an African American family dressed in their Sunday best, clearly just out of church. One of the women looked across at me, her face full of concern. "Is he okay?" she asked Kate.

While Kate answered the question, I let myself believe she was talking about someone else. Someone who lived a glamorous, adventurous life and had spent Christmas in Indonesia. Someone who had brought home a tropical disease as a souvenir and whose temperature kept spiking into the 103's. Someone who had eaten a grand total of six saltine crackers in the last week and couldn't even keep down fluids any more. Someone who felt like a stranger to me.

The woman listened, nodded, hummed sympathetically. And when Kate was done talking, the woman began-without introduction or apology-to pray for me. "Calm his system, Jesus," she said over and over again. "Calm his system, Lord."

Her voice grew more forceful, more urgent, and those around her began murmuring their assent. And as they prayed, even though

I was weak and in pain and everything was wrong, the world became right. I felt a clarity that always seems to elude me when I have my life all under control. Suddenly my God was too loving, too perfect, too beautiful, and I thought my heart would burst.

Someone in scrubs called my name just then, came over, started to wheel me away. As I left the waiting room, I could still hear the woman praying: "Calm his system, Jesus. Calm his system."

There are so many moments from my bout with dengue fever that I don't want to forget. There was the moment when I was transferred to a new floor and the nurse who greeted me said, "Welcome to the fourth floor. We have a lot of fun. We also have earplugs." There was the time my roommate, a man with psychological issues, tried to pull out his catheter and began yelling for help. There were the visits from dear friends and the daily chats with an Asian medical student named Vince. I wouldn't trade away any of these.

But best of all were the moments that can't be seen or described-the moments when God caught me by the hand and whispered, "I'm right here. I've got you. I'm never letting go."

Author: Greg Coles

I spent my childhood in Indonesia, where I tried my hand at writing, musicianship, baking, and hanging out of moving vehicles on highways. I am now a graduate student in English at Penn State.

GregColes.com

Undone

The day was warm and my belly large. The air conditioner was blowing and one second I was cold, then hot, cold, hot. The climate issue had more to do with being 4 months pregnant with my third baby than the temperature. Trees passed quickly by the car window and even though I wondered whether my nausea was going to hold off for this road trip, I was excited. I love to travel and was craving time away.

My mom's voice from the front seat carried back to me. Drifting through the sunlit air I felt the words she read wash over me. Orphans. Child Soldiers. Malnutrition. Death. Bodies Sold. Slavery. My heart began to wrench and my eyes filled with tears. Through blurred vision I saw RV's, motorcycles, brand new SUV's, huge cities and large houses fly by. My American affluence struck me hard. Financial worries and pithy dreams were laid open, bare before the stark depravity of a world in bondage. People being used and sold. Children being sold and used.

Something rose up in me and I grabbed my journal. I breathlessly started to write. I confess. I confess my ignorance and my avoidance. I confess the mis-management of wealth that has been given me. And I commit. I commit to do something. I commit that I must do something. I don't know what, but something.

That moment was the catalyst. The catalyst for a passion, the catalyst for a prayer, the catalyst for an idea. An idea about changing people's stories. An idea about each of us living the story that we were created for. Little did I know how much my story would be changed in the process.

In the months that followed, human trafficking was everywhere, how had I missed it all this time? It was across the world, across the country and right next door. Something that used to be an orphans problem in Africa suddenly became personal. These girls were my neighbors, the assailants, the people at the mall. Prostitution was no longer a lifestyle people chose but a prison that they found themselves in. I was sick to my stomach.

When we begin to pray that God will break our hearts for what breaks his we need to be ready to be broken. I had cried out from the depths that God would tune my heart to his. That I could weep with those who are weeping.

God works in steps, first awareness, awareness then leads to stirring, stirring to action and action to passion because where your time, money and energy are spent there you will find your heartbeat.

In the midst of this season, as my heart began to beat for the voiceless I experienced my own wake up call. One of my own was endangered, their life was threatened and I cried out to God, asking that he not take her from me. And he spoke back. He spoke about the thousands crying out to him from places of bondage, physical, emotional and spiritual. He spoke his heart to me, and mine broke.

I was undone. My story changed. My passion ignited. My prayers were fervent and a vision was becoming reality.

Author: Stephanie Page

Stephanie is a wife and mom to 3. Her heart is to see people living their lives on purpose for the glory of God. She spends her time as a speaker, writer, bible study leader and conference planner.

StephanieMPage.com

Let the Little Ones Come!

The sound of pee hitting the wall is unmistakable. And here's how it happens in our house: small feet rush into the bathroom, the toilet seat is thrown - thrown - up, and with an intensity known only to young children, the urine pounds the adjoining wall.

At this point I have two options. I could rush into the newly finished bathroom and shout, "What are you doing?" But that would just get me a blank stare. We all know what he's doing. Or, I could rush in, see the deer-in-the-headlights look he's giving me, take a deep breath, and commence with the cleanup.

You see, my story isn't about one experience, it's about a daily habit of choosing to be an active daddy. The fear I wrestle with is that I'll look back upon my days with my three little boys - the ones who have successively marked their territory in and around our house - and I'll realize that I spent them as an observer.

At house parties, at the park, at church, I've seen it everywhere: dads pulling away from their children because they don't know how to engage. Because their jobs are their identity. Because the video game they just downloaded feeds them with that rush of achievement more than reading Star Wars books (for the thousandth time).

But it takes prayer and planning.

In order to actually take my three year old in my arms in the morning and want to fill him up with the attention he needs, I have to center myself on Christ and decide to put myself away for awhile. And it's amazing what a difference a day makes.

If I don't prayerfully consider my children as more important than myself, than my schedule, then any time they wake up - before the sun or long after its rising - will be an inconvenient time for me. For me.

And that's just it, isn't it? What's in it for me? Where's my time? When do I get to sit on the couch and zone out?

Wiping up the mess in the bathroom (for the thousandth time) isn't what I look forward to as a dad. Sure. But those two reactions I mentioned above come from two very different places. The "What are you doing?" reaction comes from a dad who was expecting to finish the short story he was really enjoying at the moment. The deep breath-cleanup reaction comes from a dad who expects his children to be children. His children.

It's a subtle difference that takes a not-so-subtle change in my attitude. It begins when I get up before my children and pray for them. I pray that they'll learn from me how to follow in Christ's footsteps. I pray that he would show me how to follow in his footsteps. (And, in this quiet time, I take some time for myself. That's needed, too.)

That's my adventure. That's my story, every day. I either choose to serve and love my children or myself. The job of wiping down the bathroom after yet another accident isn't what I love to do, but I love the child who can't yet aim with precision.

I choose to get off the couch today and engage with the little ones. With Christ's grace flowing over me, I'll love the way he wants me to and the way my boys need me to.

Author: Ian Anderson

Husband, father, teacher, writer. Those are my titles, but my identity is in Christ. I seek to follow Him daily in each of those capacities.

FantasticReflection.blogspot.com

Adventures of a Kazakhstan Junkie

Kazakhstan.

Mountain Ranges and Plains. Apples and Tulips. Hospitality and Full Bellies. Adventures and Sweet Children's Faces. Smiles and Tears. Hamburger Surprise and Outhouses. Mosques and Mausoleums. Uno and Soccer. Birthday Celebrations and Graduations. Homemade Pizza and Movie Nights. Airplanes, Trains, Buses, Taxies, and Crazy Driving. Watermelon and Jam. Bread and More Bread. Boiled Sheep Head and Honor.

The country of Kazakhstan, located in central Asia, was the last country to receive independence from the Soviet Union in 1991. It is the largest landlocked country and the ninth largest country in the world. Kazakhstan is made up of 135 ethnic cultures including Kazkhs, Russians, Uzbeks, Udrainians, Uyghur, Tatars, and Germans. And it is this country that stole my heart the summer of 2006.

I took my first trip to Kazakhstan the summer after my junior year of high school. I traveled with ten other youth and three leaders. This was the first time the organization had allowed an all youth trip. We were ecstatic. We spent eight months preparing for the trip of a lifetime. Our main objective for the trip was to remodel a foster mother's home inside and out. After this foster mother's husband had left her and her son had died, she decided to provide a home for four orphans, and her house was in great need of repair.

Being in a developing country, we had to be a little more innovative in remodeling the home. Some of the tools we would use here in the states were not available. So instead of having a piece of equipment remove the dirt and debris out of the backyard, we had to do it. I have never worked harder than the days working there. The first two days were consumed with filling buckets of dirt and debris that had accumulated over 50+ years and dumping those buckets in a dump truck. The pile was so big we filled the dump truck four times. After the debris was removed, we then were able to put new dirt in its place. Now, the foster mother has expanded her garden to be in that space. During that same time, the kitchen was completely remodeled, repairing a decaying ceiling and sunken floor. This group of eleven teens and three leaders cleared four dump truck loads of dirt and debris out of the backyard, chopped wood, painted several rooms, the fence, and the outhouse, and completely remodeled the kitchen. The before and after pictures are incredible, if I do say so myself.

The trip was definitely not all work and no play. We had the opportunity to visit some of the mausoleums, the city museum, and a small amusement park. One of the evenings there we went to the town square. In the evenings, they block off a couple of sections of road in front of a government building and set up carnival games and food stands and photo booths and lots of other fun things.

We also had lots of delicious food! The days we were working at the foster home, the mother had a large lunch spread for us - meat and noodle dishes, cucumber and tomato salad, homemade bread and jam, fruit, and tea. It was all so delicious. And then in the middle of the afternoon she would cut up a couple of watermelons.

Many of us had been friends before this trip started, but throughout the trip we became closer than we could have ever been had we stayed in the States. There is nothing like 30 hours of travel and culture shock and strange foods and lots of hard work to bond people together.

Through this trip, I fell in love with the Kazakh people and their country and their culture. It was because of this rewarding trip I went back to Kazakhstan three other summers throughout my college years. Even though I am not as involved with Kazakhstan as I was in college, it never leaves me. It was because of this trip I studied communication studies in college and decided to make my career in nonprofit work. The experiences I had in that country will be with me forever and tend to affect decisions I make every day.

Author: Bethany Turner

I am a grant-writing and social media consultant with BMTmedia.org. I married the love of my life at age 22 and love (just about) every minute of it. I am an avid Ohio State Buckeyes fan.

TurnerBethany.wordpress.com

Made Perfect in My Weakness

I wouldn't have guessed 2 years ago that I'd be in Cambodia right now, feeling the warm breeze coming through our apartment windows, thinking about our Khmer friends and students that are so dear to my heart now. I'm quiet, shy, insecure - the opposite of a "people person." Certainly not someone you'd say was made for missions. But, what's awesome about our Lord is that He can take anyone - even someone like me - and place them perfectly within the work He's doing, anywhere in the world. As Paul says in 2 Corinthians 12:9-10, "His grace is sufficient for you, for His power is made perfect in weakness. Therefore, I will boast all the more gladly about my weaknesses, so that Christ's power may rest on me....For when I am weak, then I am made strong."

Growing up in church, international missions was something I always heard about, and something I've always been interested in. I never set out to act on this interest, though. I was married, had a demanding, full-time accounting job - and I didn't see myself as being the "right" person for missions. What does an Accountant, non-people person, have to offer? I was set in my ways, a germaphobe, and on top of that - someone who's not a natural with kids or people. What I wasn't realizing, though, is that we don't have to be capable, because God is capable for us.

3 years ago, I signed up for Beth Moore's Daniel study. I'd never done an extensive study like this before, and it ended up being a turning point in my life. One main takeaway was Psalm 82:3: "Defend the weak and the fatherless; uphold the cause of the poor and the oppressed." Even though I'd grown up in church, I hadn't seen this calling for Christians so clearly written out. A quote from the book Kisses from Katie, by Katie Davis, says it well: "Slowly but surely I began to realize the truth: I had loved

and admired and worshiped Jesus without actually doing what He said. I began to realize that God wanted more from me, and I wanted more of Him. He began to grow in me a desire to live intentionally, and different from anyone I had ever known."

My husband's heart was broken for missions after experiencing the Daraja Children's Choir of Africa, and long story short, that lead to us forming our non-profit, Threaded Leaf Project, where we work with Cambodian women, children, and students in need. However, at this time, we had yet to leave the comforts of home, and we knew God was calling us to do something bigger. We had heard about Cambodia from our pastor and friends, and we decided it was time to experience it first-hand.

We were excited...and nervous. My biggest personal fear was going to the orphanage. I tried to get over my not being a kid person, but the more time we spent there, the more insecure I felt. I was disappointed that I couldn't wholeheartedly embrace this new adventure that God had given me. For me, this trip wasn't all roses and butterflies - it was something that made me look deep inside myself...and to be honest, I didn't like what I saw. But, God didn't let my insecurities get in the way of His work. He believed in me, and I tried my hardest to trust and believe in Him. I knew I wanted to go back to Cambodia. I wanted to do better the next time, and I knew I would desperately need God for that.

As we made plans for our second trip, I'd had 6 months to digest the first trip, and 6 months for God to change my heart. I was nervous about going back to the orphanage. Would things be any different for me? I honestly wasn't sure.

As I was standing at the ferry landing, waiting to board and cross over to the orphanage, a group of women were making their way off the ferry. One of the ladies walked up to me, put her hand on my arm, and smiled at me. I started tearing up behind my sunglasses. I knew in my heart that this was God saying "You're still welcome here. Come and follow me. My power is made perfect in your weakness." So, I followed Him.

After we arrived at the orphanage, we noticed a new set of faces: three adorable, sweet, 7 year old triplet sisters. They were so cute, so loving. One of them attached herself to me all that day, taking me everywhere she went, holding my hand, smiling and laughing as we ran and played. I knew without a doubt that God had connected us that day. Her love changed my heart...HIS love changed my heart.

This is when I knew Cambodia was where God wanted us.

Today, we now spend extensive time in Cambodia working on our clothing and accessories lines, visiting the orphanage, spending time with our scholarship students, and visiting with the other lifelong friends we've made along the way.

Isn't it awesome how God so beautifully orchestrates things in our lives? God has taught me that He has a plan for my life, and that He loves me enough to pursue me. He's taught me that I need not question Him, even when I don't understand why He would use me in His plans. I am eternally grateful to Him.

So please take this away with you: He has a perfect plan for your life. Stepping out of your comfort zones, both mentally and physically, is worth it. Beth Moore wrote, "No amount of comfort is worth missing the greatest adventure humankind can experience." Thank you, Father, that You really are made perfect in our weakness. Thank you for the abundant joy You give us as we get up off our couches to follow You.

Author: Karen McCown

I'm the Treasurer, Designer, and Lifelong Partner of Threaded Leaf Project, a non-profit working to improve the lives of students, women, and children in Cambodia. I love the life I get to lead!

ThreadedLeafProject.org

Fully Surrendered. Abundantly Blessed

The warm, moist air surrounds me. Scents of rain mingled with exhaust fumes and tropical flowers and fruits permeate my senses. My life is amazing. Some days are better than others. Some are spent soaking my pillow with tears of homesickness as I realize that my family is thousands of miles away from me. Some are spent on my knees in adoration of my King. Some are spent rejoicing in His goodness and faithfulness. But each tear I cry, each smile that lights up my face, and every craving for American peanut butter reminds me of how incredibly blessed I am. This is the story of my life, scripted by a masterful Author.

My life as a 12-year-old was normal enough. Being raised in a God-fearing family with amazing parents and 3 incredible brothers, I felt quite comfortable with my life as it was. Jesus was my delight and my joy. I had a room of my own, running water, hot showers, a pantry and refrigerator stocked with food, and 20 acres of land to enjoy. My days were spent doing normal things that any 12-year-old would do, but one of my favorite times was when my brothers and I went to youth group at our church. On one such night the Lord decided to come and gently move me out of my comfort zone.

My eyes blurred as tears began to stream down my face. A few of my hot tears fell onto the pages of the Book that I was reading. I had just gotten home from youth group and went straight to my room as I felt the Lord tugging on my heart to listen to what He wanted to say to me. Dropping my bag by my door, I reached for my Bible and sat at my desk ready and expectant for the Lord to speak to me. He led me to read Isaiah 61. "The Spirit of the Sovereign Lord is upon me, because the Lord has anointed me to bring good news to the poor...."

"My daughter, that is you. Go, I am sending YOU and anointing YOU."

I know God's word was not written to us but for us. This passage was about Jesus but indirectly I felt that to follow Jesus I too had to be His disciple and be ready to be used by Him. I continued to read.

"...He has sent me to bind up the brokenhearted, to proclaim liberty to the captives, and the opening of the prison to those who are bound..."

He continued to speak.

"Go, my Beloved. Would you be My missionary to the ends of the earth?"

As my tears flowed, I answered Him from the quiet place in my soul. "Yes, God, I will go for You. Here I am, send me." The sweet time with my Lord that night forever changed me.

A few months later my dad brought my family to the country of the Philippines for a 2 week mission trip with the organization CMC (Church Multiplication Coalition) doing church-planting, evangelism, and praying for the sick. Our plane arrived on the beautiful island of Cebu. The cabin door opened, and passengers began to file out the door. My family and I, as weary and jet-lagged as we were, excitely bounded out of the plane. The sticky, tropical air filled our nostrils as our feet touched the warm asphalt. A strange sensation swept over my body when my feet touched the ground. It was a feeling of arriving after a long journey and stepping inside to the familiar environment of your home. A feeling of peace and love for the Filipino people flooded my heart, and a thought formulated in my mind:

"I am home."

Having never been outside of America before, I wasn't sure where this thought or strange feeling had come from. So, setting aside those thoughts and feelings, I enjoyed our mission trip. It was 2 weeks full of learning a new culture, stepping out of my comfort zone to preach in churches and evangelize to strangers, meeting new friends and eating strange foods. (ever tried balut? Look it up.) Many tears were shed as we said goodbye to our Filipino friends after the 2 weeks had come to an end. The plane ride back to America was a sad one because I was filled with a feeling that only the word "homesickness" can describe. I truly missed the Philippines and had an intense desire to go back to a country that I had fallen in love with.

One year later, in 2009, my dad brought us back to the Philippines, and again every year after that. Each trip brought me back to that sweet night with the Lord when I was 12 years old. I graduated high school in 2012 and took another trip with my family to the Philippines that summer. Halfway through our time there, the Lord spoke to me during my quiet time with Him.

"Daughter, I have placed a love for this country in your heart for a reason. Come back this November and live here."

After praying and seeking His confirmation (and with my my parents' blessing), I packed my suitcases and boarded a plane with 3 other young ladies nearly one month after my 18th birthday. We are interns under CMC, an organization that plants multiplying churches in nations around the world. Some days I look around at the beautiful scenery, the brown-skinned people with smiles that fill their faces, and the cute little bamboo huts, and I pinch myself. I must be dreaming. Nope. A quick peek outside reminds me that I am still here. Still in this beautiful country that I now call my {earthly} home. Still here, exactly where He wants me. I am no longer satisfied with being "normal" or living an ordinary life. My contentment is found in surrendering my life to Him.

A life fully surrendered to the Lord, with no turning back, is an abundantly blessed life.

Author: Rebecca Kinabrew

I have fallen in love with Someone named Jesus. My smile, my joy, my everything is wrapped up in Him. It is my delight and joy to take His Gospel to the ends of the earth.

His-Etcetera.blogspot.com

Trailer Park Christmas Caroling

Every Friday morning I had been going to my friend Robert's trailer for a breakfast with a local ministry. They're working to build a healthy community with the formerly homeless in a trailer park out by the airport.

A few weeks ago I was talking with Aaron. He's a quiet man, with a huge belly, who waits an awkward 10 seconds before making any response to your questions, but has a wonderful sense of humor making me laugh out loud in surprise. I asked Aaron if they ever had carolers in the trailer park in an attempt at conversation while we were waiting for the eggs Nick and Lisa were cooking. After the usual awkward time gap, he replied, "Not that I recall," in his deep slow voice. So I casually mentioned that we should all go caroling.

Will, a man with deep set wrinkles around his eyes due to years of smoking, grey scraggly hair past his shoulders, and the giver of the best hugs you'll ever receive, overheard and decided that this is what we should do.

So it was decided. Sunday night. 7:00.

Robert made a nice pot of decaf coffee and had warm brownies on the stove when I arrived.

Rosa was already there donned with her bright red Christmas sweater and quick wit. Then Josie and Tom trickled in and I called Will to make sure he was on his way.

Josie and Tom are the newly weds of the group. Josie has a

smile that, despite the fact that she is missing many of her front teeth, will brighten up any room. Her smiles seem to be few and far between these days as she finds herself continually drawn back to the street in her addiction - to the heartbreak of her husband. Tom hobbles at her side due to an incident a few months ago when he was high and jumped off a building to impress his bride, but manages to get around okay these days.

We decided to sing a bit in Robert's trailer to see what we were working with. I think we sounded beautiful.

Robert and Will had procured hymnals to help us with the more obscure verses of Away in a Manger and we set out with candles in hand because I insisted that "real" carolers hold candles. Turns out that we wouldn't have been able to see without them.

As we walked to the first house Rosa quickly realized that she needed to be wearing her glasses to read from the hymnal, but needed to not be wearing her glasses to walk. Quite the predicament when you're trying to read carol lyrics and walk simultaneously. So we ingeniously decided to sing songs we knew as we walked and save the more lyrically difficult songs to when we were in front of a trailer.

There we were, walking/hobbling through the streets of the trailer park armed with candles and hymnals. Our first stop with an audience was Alabama's trailer. Alabama has the most wonderful deep voice that speaks with authority and dignity. As we sang, I couldn't stop staring at Alabama's wide smile as he listened to our haphazard melodies. After our first verse of Joy to the World, Alabama commented incredulously, "You pulled it off." Someone handed him a candle and he joined our parade to Jonny's trailer.

Once we arrived, Jonny invited us in. We took up his entire living room/kitchen/dining room and we proceeded to sing while some bad rendition of a Victorian novel blared on the TV and his two newest lovebirds chirped incessantly. Although Jonny isn't always all there mentally, he has the biggest heart and is the kindest friend you'll find.

Jonny joined us and we headed to Aaron's trailer. Aaron grinned all through our off key Fa-la-la-las and when asked if he wanted to join us, replied with a matter of fact "No thank you" with no further explanation. But he did watch us walk all the way down the street with a big smile on his face.

On to Hector. Upon completion of our first carol amidst their small dogs attacking our ankles, Robert asked Hector if he had any requests. He said no and that one song was enough. Perhaps we didn't sound quite as beautiful to an outside ear.

Having made the rounds, we headed back to Robert's for a bit more coffee. Our group now multiplied, we pulled out the folding chairs and everyone took up their usual seats from Friday breakfasts. Robert asked us to share favorite Christmas stories and it was a jolly time of sharing and remembering.

As I left, Jonny gave me an uncharacteristic hug. Rosa mentioned that she doesn't have many friends and that we should hang out when I get back from the holidays. Tom and Josie invited me to stop by their trailer any time.

I had made connections with all of these friends at the breakfasts, but something was different this time. It felt like I was tearing something away as I left. Like I belonged there with them, but I was leaving to go back to my little apartment across town.

I may have had a tear or two run down my cheek as I drove

away.

Will called me the next evening to tell me that I had made his Christmas. Next time someone asks him to share his favorite Christmas story, he told me, he's going to tell the one of us caroling.

I think I will too.

Note - names have been changed

Author: Jen Lewis

Jen owns an online Fair Trade handbag boutique, Purse & Clutch, to help create jobs for artisans in developing countries with limited opportunities.

PurseandClutch.com

David Lee

A buddy called me up one day....

Buddy: "Brian, let's go to McDonalds...get some cheeseburgers...and drive around downtown Wichita looking for some homeless people."

Me: "Yup!"

We decided to get 2 cheeseburgers and hand them out to two different homeless downtowners. I was a little hesitant...definitely out of my comfort zone. We decided the first homeless person we saw would be the one. The first corner we turned we found David. He was walking towards us with his entire wealth stuffed in a trash-bag, being carried over his shoulder. You could see it in his face. Tired. Hungry. Stuck. We'd soon learn that he used to live a few states away and through crazy circumstances landed in the middle of America on his own with nothing but what he could carry on his back. But we wouldn't find this out today.

We pulled over and went chasing after him. When we caught up to him he was rolling tobacco in some paper he had obviously found in the trash. We asked him if he was hungry.... I don't think it was until after we asked that we felt like idiots. But he was nice and verified that, yes...tobacco smoked from paper trash wasn't his idea of a healthy lunch. (Not that the McDonalds cheeseburger was a listed item on the Paleo diet.) It was hard to understand his words because of his lack of dental hygiene, but it was easy to understand his countenance. He was lost and didn't care. He was defeated and a little angry. We didn't quite know what to say so after some small talk and explaining that we were giving him lunch in the name of Jesus...who gives much more than a cheeseburger to the hungry....we turned and walked away. We gave him both cheeseburgers.

Walking away I felt a pretty cool energy I had not felt in a long time. There is a compounding energy linked to serving others that is contagious when it is initiated. I had motivation to do this again. We decided we would repeat this in a few days.

Two days later my buddy called me up again. We met at McDonalds, grabbed a few cheeseburgers and got in the car. We went a different way as if we were somehow trying to avoid David. Spread the love, right? First street no one. Next street, David.

How could we not stop and say hi to him?! We again chased him down, hoping he'd remember us. He did...I think...but it definitely wasn't as cool for him as it was for us. This time we got his story. He had a wife and kids, he had lost his job and subsequently lost touch with his family. There were a lot of details I don't remember, but I do remember that he was trying to get to Denver, CO. He said that he knew of a place that was a shelter for the homeless and had programs to help them hit the "Refresh" button. It was the only moment that he showed excitement for life. We prayed for him to find his way there and bid adieu. This time we walked away feeling like we were ignoring his need. Was this an opportunity we were being given to make a difference in someone's life?

Now we had a mission. We met again the next day, got the merchandise and went searching. Guess how hard it was to find David? I think it took three minutes. This time he seemed happy to see us, as if now we were familiar faces to him. We gave him the cheeseburgers which at this point was a secondary exchange. My buddy had gone home and gathered some clothes and a backpack he didn't need anymore. He was about the same height as David and the thought was to give him a new wardrobe. He was very thankful to have newer clothes and a real bag to carry them in. But the primary reason we were there was to ask him a question.

"David, how would you like to go to Denver?"

We explained to him that we had a train ticket to Denver with his name on it. We had letters with pre-stamped envelopes and return addresses to us so he could write. We had contacted the organization in Denver and had the location for him to get there. Not sure of his reaction, we stood anxious for his response...and it was filled with excitement. Now he couldn't stop thanking us and talking about what he was going to do when he got there. My friend told him to meet him at the train station downtown the next day and he would see him off (I had to work). I got the call from my buddy the next day that David was headed to Denver. He couldn't stop thanking my friend for the opportunity we had given him. We were so excited to hear from him and know that he was back on his feet soon.

It was the last time we ever heard from him. We assume he most likely used the paper and envelopes to smoke some more tobacco. Or he got off the train at a different location. Or he just joined the massive homeless population in Denver and got back in his comfort zone. But a part of us feels like we made a difference. That we helped a broken, defeated old man find new life. New energy to hit the "Refresh" button... and maybe even get reconciled with his family. Although we will never know what happened to David, I can hold on to a lesson learned: serving others is contagious. Helping others feels a thousand times better than helping ourselves. And if you can't find the courage to do it alone, grab a friend. Adding helpers exponentially adds to the help that is being provided.

Hopefully the stories in this book will be all the evidence you need.

Author: Brian Gensch

I am a husband, a son, a brother, an uncle, a musician, an athlete-ish, a wealth advisor, and most importantly a child of God. I have tons of skills. I am 30 years old. I am mostly bald.

Be Willing

One of the gifts I've discovered over the years is that God has an amazing ability to work through us and in us when we simply choose to be receptive to where He is leading.

Years ago, God nudged me to sign up to be a part of the mission team at the church I was attending. I had never done anything like that before. As someone who likes her little routine environment this was a big leap into the unknown. Yet I had seen, over and over in my life, the evidence of what God is capable of accomplishing when we are simply willing to go.

When we are weak. He is strong. Each time I've chosen to obey and move when He says move I've discovered this to be one of the beautiful results of obedience. God is faithful to show up and give us the strength we need to do the task He calls us to do.

I rejoice each time I think about how this once timid girl, who was terrified to speak in public, was prompted to start a recovery group at her church. And God brought people there every week to find healing and comfort from their hurts, habits, and hangups.

And, the first time I boarded a plane to Dominican Republic (DR) I was just as nervous to step into a new environment where I felt completely unqualified. My only desire was to be willing to serve and give back to others. We would be painting at the school our church helps to support, visiting our sponsored children, visiting the orphanage, and delivering rice and beans.

One of the most unexpected moments on that whole trip was the day we delivered rice and beans. The pastor we partner with in the DR took us up into the mountains to some of the neediest families in the area. With backpacks filled with food, we moved from house to house giving away our gift.

I will never forget the lady who disappeared back into her house to retrieve a gift for us. Bananas. We didn't want to take her food, but she insisted. She wanted us to have them.

Years ago I chose to step into the unknown. I loved it so much I chose to go back two more years after that. And each time I did, God opened my eyes to the incredible beauty that stretches out beyond my safe little world.

I was willing and God was faithful to do the rest...just like always!

Author: Eileen Knowles

Eileen Knowles lives in North Georgia. She is passionate about leaving a legacy for her son and encouraging others along the way who might need a dose of hope poured into their weary lives.

EileenKnowles.com

Great < Good

I grew up watching a brilliant TV show called "Boy Meets World." Although the show was chock-full of great one-liners and the comedic brilliance that was the Feeny call, one of the final scenes of the show still vividly sticks with me today. Right before the gang leaves Mr. Feeny's classroom for the last time, America's favorite teacher/principal/professor/neighbor offers Cory, Shawn, and the rest of humanity one final Feeny-ism:

Feeny: Believe in yourselves. Dream. Try. Do good.
Topanga: Don't you mean, "Do well"?
Feeny: No, I mean do good.

This "Boy Meets World" generation also grew up in a culture that coached and inspired us to achieve greatness. We do believe in ourselves. We're not afraid to dream or try. In fact, we almost believe in ourselves to a fault. We think we can do whatever we want if we work hard enough. We may not verbalize it, but most of us see the success of LeBron James and Justin Bieber and other young superstars and think, "I could do that. I'm good enough to compete at their level. I have what it takes to be great."

Everyone is good. Good isn't good enough. We yearn for greatness.

Although Topanga attempted to educate George Feeny about the difference between "well" and "good," most of us make a similar argument about goodness vs. greatness. This underlying issue drove the plot of the Wizard of Oz reboot, "Oz: The Great and Powerful." After what we assume to be years of mediocrity, Oscar Diggs explains, "I don't want to be a good man... I want to be a great one." You can almost hear the years of pain and disappointment in his voice; the same pain that almost everyone in our generation feels as we get older.

We don't want to do well. Good isn't good enough. We need to be called "great."

Recently I had the chance to apply for a job that made me feel great. A very large and very successful organization had an opening that at first glance seemed like a custom-fit for me. I went through the application process and ended up being one of their final two candidates. After a nation-wide search of very qualified and unbelievably talented candidates, it was beginning to feel like this was it. This was my chance to show people I was great. In all of my 24-year-old wisdom, I told myself I had worked long enough at a good job. I was ready for something great.

By the end of my final interview, I was well aware that I was not ready for the job. I'm good at what I do and I probably would have done well in the role, but it wasn't right at this time for several different reasons. One of them, even though I didn't want to admit it, was my attitude and my perspective. The dream of a cool title at a successful company inspired me to show off the best I had to offer. My desire for greatness outweighed my desire for goodness.

Our culture today (probably more than ever before) idolizes young success stories. We love Mark Zuckerberg and Blake Mycoskie and Justin Timberlake and the like. If we are young and talented but have yet to be on the cover of Wired or GQ, it's strangely easy to feel like a failure. We feel like something is wrong with us if we don't have 1000 Twitter followers. We should be better than this, we think. By now we should be better than ourselves.

Interestingly enough, many great people aren't very good, and many very good people aren't very great.

The more we focus on wealth and fame and success and pleasure, the less we tend to focus on our spouses and our children and our communities-and even ourselves.

As a Christian, I follow a Man who made radical claims like "The last will be first, and the first will be last." The "last" are often the ones who strive for goodness; most of the "firsts" strive for greatness.

The rest of the world may never understand, but let's be a generation that yearns to do good instead of being great. Never make excuses for poor work and continue to be the best at what you do. But at the same time, remember to use your skills and gifts on things that matter. Yes, the Bible teaches this, but deep down you know that this kind of life is more meaningful-even if you don't believe the rest of the Bible.

Besides. As a rule of thumb, it's generally a good idea to take advice from Mr. Feeny.

Author: Matt Ehresman

Matt Ehresman likes to write, design, film and create a lot of stuff. He also consumes large quantities of Mountain Dew and enjoys super hero movies. He lives with his wife, Tillie, in Kansas.

MattEhresman.com

The Power of the Simple Words,
"I am so sorry"

The last student walked out of my classroom and left it empty of people and noise, both of which had become balms to my broken heart. Noise, not ice cream, had become the thing that I had tried to "fill up" my life with since the unexpected and devastating break up with my fiancé. Noise, and my desire for companionship, drove me to play countless episodes of old TV shows until I fell asleep at night. Morning talk shows were what I blasted, from the first moments of rising each morning, they kept me "company" in the early hours of my day and taught me more pop culture than I had ever known in my life.

This drove me to throw myself into my teaching career as never before. I arrived at the school at 6:00 a.m. most mornings and left approximately thirteen to eighteen hours later. So far, outside of my family and best friends, no one seemed to notice. Most of the adults that I worked with seemed unsure of what to say, and with that came stilted conversations and lots of awkward silence. What I wanted, and what my heart desperately needed, was for someone to care enough to say they were sorry. I longed for someone to see beyond the broken shell of a person that I had become. I longed to see love acted out in human form.

This unspoken prayer request was about to come in the most unsuspecting answer: through my students.

Needing a distraction from the silence I walked out of my room and wandered down the hallway to the 3rd floor lounge, which had huge picture windows that overlooked the soccer field. As I settled into a chair I surveyed the still winter scene outside and sardonically thought about how similar this was to my life. As I

220

sat pondering life I didn't hear "P", one of my senior students come in and settle in on a chair beside me. As it dawned on me that he was there I felt the teacher side of me kick in and looked for something "brilliant" to say. Through my own pain I was dimly aware that the holidays must have been just as difficult for "P" as they were for me, due to some family situations, but could think of nothing to say.

"This view is amazing. I never get tired of it." I heard "P" say. I replied something of an agreement and then sighed.

"How was your holiday, Ms. V"? He asked.

"Short." I replied. My voice was laced with frustration and sadness. I had only been back in Maryland for three days and my family, in Tennessee, seemed thousands of miles away. It seemed like I had been back in Maryland for years.

"Ms. V -" He interrupted my thoughts and I turned to look at him as I realized he was hesitating. "Ms. V" he said again. "I am so sorry." As I glanced away and then back at the young man sitting beside me I realized that my cheeks were wet with silent tears.

"Thank you." I whispered.

For the first time someone outside my family and best friends had acknowledged the pain I was going through. Not in a way of making it better but with four simple words that acknowledged the deep hurt I was feeling and gave me room to grieve. Those four precious words were uttered from someone who had done nothing to cause the pain but instead chose to step into the pain. I am not sure how long we sat there that day before the bell rang. I do remember the feeling of peace filling that room because a senior decided to look outside of themselves and reach out to their teacher whose life had been seemingly shattered. It's ironic because in many ways nothing changed that day, but in other ways everything changed. The need for noise to numb the pain was gone and within it was replaced a peace that had been lost since the night my life had been shattered.

It has been four years and those students became college graduates last month. It has been four years, and yet I am reminded of that year often with simple gratitude.

Often times all we need is someone to come and sit with us and simply say "I am so sorry". It might seem like it is not enough but trust me- it can change everything. The minute you choose to extend grace and kindness to another hurting human being something powerful happens.

That year was living proof of this to me. As time went on there were countless ways that love was physically expressed by this senior class. At a time that could understandably have been one of the most selfish times in their lives, these seniors poured love into my life. There were hundreds of letters of encouragement, students who convinced me to take up running after school, little notes left on my desk, in books, and on my car, CD's made that were filled with uplifting music, DVD's given, a lovely lady that called me "beautiful" when I looked anything but, invitations to eat lunch with them so that I never ate alone, many jokes and pranks played that brought laughter, Starbucks gift cards, money for a new car when my car died, invitations to weekend outings (including Valentine's Day) and hundreds of Dutch Blitz games simply because I said I liked it. Whether it was a conspiracy, or a simple plan to care, these simple yet precious acts of love changed my life.

What could have been the worst year of my life I truly only remember with a fond and humble smile. A circumstance that brought me so much pain was the backdrop for a beautiful time in my life.

And it all started with the powerful and yet simple words of "I am so sorry".

Author: Rebecca VanDeMark

I am a writer, teacher, speaker, and blogger who loves Jesus, life, the concept of hope, and all things pretty as I survive and thrive with advanced late stage lymes disease and cancer.

Caravansonnet.com

Love in a Green Skirt

When I thought about being a missionary, I thought about doing something great. Changing the world, making a difference, feeling connected, seeing results.

Instead, when we went to the Solomon Islands, I changed diapers. I made dinner. I felt depressed. And there was no end in sight.

Our neighbors were so kind to me and my husband, so precious to our kids. And yet I wanted more. I wanted to know and be known. To share my heart and have someone share theirs in return. But the language and cultural barriers were immense. And I just couldn't get past wishing for the kind of relationships that made sense to me.

One Saturday afternoon when I was feeling especially depressed, my husband and I went for a walk along the beach. Because even I had been known to cheer up on the beach.

We met up with an old lady down at the beach, wearing a bright green skirt and nothing else. Breasts hanging down to her waist, tattoos in between her breasts.

As soon as she saw me, she cried out with pleasure: "Oh my daughter, oh my daughter."

I have never, in our ten years here, had anyone call me by a kinship term; I hardly knew how to respond. Was she really calling me her daughter? But she didn't just say it once-she kept repeating it.

She put both arms around me and hugged me. I've had plenty of women hold my hand out here, but I've never, ever had anybody hug me. She went on and on, talking and laughing, holding my hand, so happy that I was there.

While I, of course, was doing nothing spectacular-not witnessing, not leading a Bible study. I was there, doing nothing, saying nothing, just there.

And she was thrilled. As if she delighted in me, just because I was there.

Every time I think of her, I am reminded of Elijah, under his broom tree, telling God to go ahead and let him die. I think about Elijah, so tired and alone, no longer asking for a blessing, just asking for an end. Seeing great things happen through him, and too exhausted to ask for anything to happen in him. And the angel came and touched Elijah.

And I always think that this lady was my angel, with her hard old hands and her great soft breasts and her tattoos and her pipe of tobacco and her pleasure at my existence. And I realize that, like Elijah's angel, she was the answer to a prayer I hadn't even had the heart to pray.

Author: Kay Bruner

I'm a wife, mom, friend, and therapist, learning to live as God's beloved.

KayBruner.com

Lies That Tie: Fear Will Keep You on the Couch

Hot, slippery tears poured down my cheeks as I curled into a ball on the dorm bed. The nostalgic surroundings invited palpable memories to surface as deja vu ricocheted around the barren room. I could almost see the last nine years of transformation rewinding before me. Suddenly, I was no longer a 29-year-old on a humid August day in 2012; I was once again a fear-ridden 20-year-old in 2003, fighting for truth to grip my life.

I know all too well how fear can tie you to the couch. That yellow-striped love seat, appropriately faded for a college dorm room, sits in my mind's eye like the figurative picture that it is. Situated under an old wooden window, it offered an easy escape from the world out there...the world where people looked and people judged and comparisons were made and shortcomings seemed to gleam in naked exposure. That world was terrifying to me, and that terror drove me to the couch.

The hurts that led to the fear began my freshman year of college when my former high school boyfriend spoke words that drove spikes deep into my heart. His words, though intended to explain his actions, sank into deep places of my soul and festered, turning into lies about myself that I chose to believe. The truth I knew about my worth in Christ became abstract while the toxic lines of rhetoric that I recited to myself seemed to become reality. The ensuing struggle intensified over the next few years until I had moments, and even days, when I virtually loathed myself.

This self-despising reached a climax my junior year of college. I lived in a quaint little dorm on campus with a wonderful roommate who had been my friend since the beginning of my time at John Brown University. Her friendship, like so many other friendships from that time, presents a strange irony to me. Though much of my college experience was riddled with paralyzing insecurity and a sense of inferiority, it was somehow graced with amazing friends and endearing memories. Looking back, I see the goodness of God even in the midst of my defeat.

As my junior year unfolded, the lies about myself became so firmly rooted that I found myself trapped in incessant comparison. "I'm not as thin as...", "I'm not as beautiful as...", "I'm not as disciplined as...", "I'm not as vibrant as...", "I'll never be as...", etc. Such rancid thoughts took up residence in my mind like nagging pests. Though I knew the Lord and wanted to please Him, the continual circuit of lies that imprisoned my heart kept me from a life of true freedom and victory.

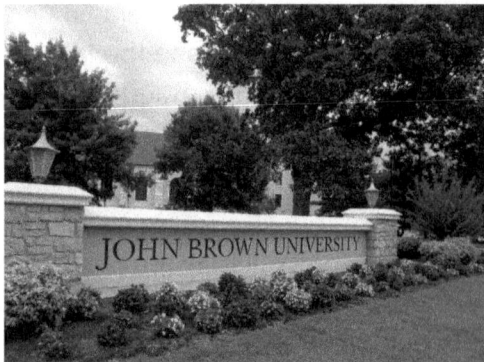

I remember so many weekend nights that year when my friends would venture out to some social gathering and, like the cripple I had become, I would choose to stay in the dorm by myself. If the situation were safe enough, then I might dare to join, but I was not about to dive into an environment where the comparison circuit would crank up and my insecurities would squeeze the breath out of me. No, thanks. The comfort of that proverbial couch was way more inviting. That couch wouldn't judge me. That couch wouldn't draw out my fears. That couch seemed like a haven from the storm.

Yet, that was exactly the problem. That couch wasn't really a haven. It was only a crutch. It didn't provide answers or healing or clarity or truth. It only provided a temporary relief. I wish someone had told me that in 2003. I wish that I could have seen the bondage I had to that couch. I wish I could re-do that year of college, and the years before when the foundation of lies were sown.

In light of such regret, Paul's words in Philippians 3:13-14 become incredibly poignant: "Brothers, I do not consider myself yet to have taken hold of it. But one thing I do: Forgetting what is behind and straining toward what is ahead, I press on toward the goal to win the prize for which God has called me heavenward in Christ Jesus." The failures of the past do not have to be a hindrance to me now. Through Christ's strength, I can forget what is behind and keep my face set on where I am headed. This is a glorious truth.

In small and yet miraculous ways, God began to restore truth to my heart after that tempetuous junior year. That summer I devoted myself to regaining health and learning to believe God at His Word. Since then, my life has continued to be transformed by the life-giving truth of Scripture and by the faithfulness that God has shown in His dealings with me. I am a living testament that God's faithfulness "reaches to the skies." (Psalm 57:10).

Over the last nine years, that couch has continued to shrink. The flood of tears that fell on that bright August day just last summer spoke my gratefulness for the grace of God in my life. That day, I sat on a dorm bed on the campus of my alma mater, with my roommate from that challenging junior year sitting by my side. We had both traveled back to our college town to celebrate the wedding of a dear friend, and we just so happened to be sharing a room in the dorms during our time there.

Sitting there on that bed, sobs erupted as I told my friend how sorry I was for that junior year of hiding and fear. She rubbed my back and spoke words of forgiveness. I sobbed because I felt a level of regret, but I sobbed out of joy that God has and is continuing to work His redemption story in me. I sobbed tears of thanks for a living God who pulls His children off the couch.

He pulled me off and He can pull you off too.

Author: Jessica Naramore

I am a middle school music teacher in Colorado Springs who loves to drink coffee, sit by fireplaces, hike, ski, discover the depths of God's grace, and learn from the stories of people around me.

MyLifeinLayers.blogspot.com

Through the Lense

In her first interview after joining the team, Mary* would not look up. Speaking via a Kenyan sign language interpreter she kept her eyes downcast, and signed short responses to the questions about her past. We learned she was nineteen and had one daughter. She came from up country and has not been working. At the end of the interview, when asked if she liked working with Sasa Designs by the Deaf, she looked up and smiled for the first time. We were overjoyed to welcome her to the team.

In the following week I saw her retreat to a downcast state. She did her work with care, making intricately beaded bracelets and submitting them to the Deaf team leader for approval. Still, she didn't interact much with the rest of the team at tea time, and she was reserved during lunch time. I asked my colleagues what the rest of her story was. I learned that about two years before she had been gang-raped by a group of men in her slum, leaving her pregnant with twins. One of the babies had died at birth.

Now a deaf, single mom, Mary was still recovering from the trauma and looking for an opportunity to move ahead. I was taking pictures a few days later at a work event, and she shyly asked to see my camera. At first she held it upside down, struggling to understand what piece of the mechanics she was supposed to look at or through. After I helped her she took her first few photos. An enormous smile emerged as the photo appeared on the digital screen. I let her take the camera and she spent the next half hour running around the event taking pictures of her colleagues, the visiting community, and a number of the children. I had never seen her so energetic.

When Mary brought the camera back, she carefully handed it to me and signed "thank you." Later, as I reviewed the photos I marveled at the woman I had glimpsed that day. A woman who beyond her deafness and her trauma, was yearning to explore the world and discover her place in it. While we cannot address her history solely by giving her a job, we hope that we have given her a new lens through which to see her future and escape the damage of her past.

Name changed to honor the privacy of the individual.

Author: Megan McDonald

I'm a world wanderer putting down roots wherever I go! With a background in non-profit, government and social enterprise, I manage a job creation project for Deaf women just outside Nairobi, Kenya.

Sasadesignsbythedeaf.com

Old Eyes, New Sight: Because Compassion Knows No Age

He had never been to a church like that one. It was a building, all right, just like any building with four walls and a roof, chairs, and even a platform up front for the preacher to preach. It had windows and a door and a wooden floor. But the walls were made of unpainted cinder blocks and the chairs were the plastic lawn variety, bent and flimsy, dirty and used up. Still, it held the rain and wind at bay and provided a comfortable place to worship. Adequate enough. Better than many other places he'd heard about. It was not the building itself that shook him to the core. It was the people who came through the doors.

We had been in Ecuador for a few days on a mission trip. We had come with the specific goal of painting a seminary that trains theological students from four different Andean countries. He had come to help cook meals for the workers. It was his first mission trip even though he was 73 and had been in ministry for many years. But he said he just had to come. His heart was on this trip from the moment it was announced. And even though he felt old and unprepared and scared, he knew he had to be there.

He and I stood at the entrance of the church that afternoon watching people go by and inviting them to come in to the soon-to-begin service. He noticed right away the unpaved road with a stream of water sneaking downhill. He asked the pastor if there were busted pipes somewhere uphill. The pastor smiled wistfully and explained that this neighborhood had no pipes. No sewer system to speak of, really. A frown crossed his brow.

"People still live like this?" he asked me.

"Worse," I said.

And then the children came.

We had advertised puppets and a hot meal so the children came in hordes. We packed probably close to two hundred people in the church on that cool evening. The children were filthy. Filthy faces, filthy clothes, filthy little bodies. My nose betrayed me after a while and I went to step outside to catch a breath of fresh air. That's where I found him. He was leaning against the doorframe facing the backs of the children, watching them raise their hands in praise as they sang, giggled at the puppets, answered questions in unison, and behaved like children should anywhere in the world. I smiled up at him thinking he was enjoying it, and then I saw it. His face was covered in tears that would not stop flowing. His lips were trembling and his eyes looked pained.

"I never knew poverty like this existed," he said. "And I never knew people with so little could be so happy. And I have so much..." he choked and could not continue.

He told me later, that evening was a defining moment for him. His heart broke that night and pieces of it stayed in that church with those children. He has not been the same since. He came back to his country, to his small Southern town, to his life as a retired minister, a changed man. He sees the world through different eyes now. And it shows in what he is choosing to do with his time. He volunteers to help children after school in one of the most impoverished areas of our city. He takes the leftover food from our church's weekly meals to families in need. He is giving his life away to reach those in need. He may never be able to go overseas again. He is getting older after all, he says. But those seven days spent among the physically poor, but spiritually, rich taught him more than decades of ministry in a first world country ever did.

Compassion is not ageist. It doesn't care if you are retired and it doesn't believe there is an age limit to give and to serve. It will take hold of you in your seventies because it is never too late to become a couch rebel.

Author: Gaby Johnson

Gaby is a wife and mother of two. She writes about adoption, parenting and faith. She spends her days homeschooling her kids, working from home, and loving her husband, while neglecting her house.

TheJohnsonGlassHouse.blogspot.com

The Moment

We had a moment, my son and I.

Home from Serbia, his country of origin, just three months, we are still dancing around one another trying to find our place in the other's heart. There are days when I feel he still ignores me, like I am at the bottom on the list of desired playmates, helpers, family members. There are days when I wonder where he comes from and I cannot place him in my frame of reference, so foreign he continues to seem.

I have born an infant into this family on seven separate occasions, but this is my first time melding a child with a past, a three-year history I know little about, into our lives. What we do know is hard to take. Rejected and abandoned simply because of the extra chromosome that gives him those tell-tale characteristics of Down syndrome. Alone in the hospital for months following an open heart surgery with apparent complications, he was left with a long, jagged physical scar and certain, but subtle, emotional scars, as well.

People thought we were nuts, leaving behind seven to pursue one we knew so little about. "How can you handle so many kids? What if he doesn't fit with the others? What if he's diseased or extra delayed?" Or my own secret fears, "What if I don't love him?" or worse, "What if I love and love and he never loves me back?"

So many times throughout the arduous process, I wanted to flee, to put a stop to it, to acknowledge with everyone else that this is crazy! But I was compelled by the knowledge that God had said go, and that this little boy needed us. So we went.

Meeting him, holding him for the first time, breathing him in was glorious and right. We bonded well initially, but upon arrival home, I was unexpectedly hospitalized with kidney stones and infection. I'm sure in his mind, I disappeared and he was abandoned once again. He withdrew. Those early fears of mine seemed to become reality as he retreated from my attempts to love him.

But more and more he is present, actively aware of what is happening in the broader scope of his surroundings, versus the three foot window to which he allowed himself to attend those first weeks home. I used to be soundly ignored by him when I'd walk in the door from work and attempt to interact. Then, ever so subtly, I sensed a change, and soon my son would smile when he saw the excitement of his siblings upon my return.

I was pleased, but didn't get too excited knowing, as I did, that he was simply feeding off the glee around him.

But yesterday it happened.

I pulled in the driveway and saw him in the window watching the car. I waved through the windshield and received no response, no flicker of recognition, no knowing smirk, just blankness. Disappointed, but not surprised, I opened my door and stepped out. I looked up at him and saw his face transform.

Ever so slowly, the corners of his mouth pulled until he had the hugest grin, the kind that makes his eyes disappear, and he pressed his head to the glass and banged on the window as he continued to smile at me with joy, as if to say, "Momma's home! Look, everyone! Momma's home!"

Tears sprang to my eyes and my breath caught in my throat as I waved. It is an incredible feeling to be known by one you've worked so hard to love.

He knows me! And, judging by his reaction, I think he even likes me.

I went upstairs after greeting the rest of the crew and found him strumming (pounding, poking, picking) his sister's guitar that he found laying on the floor of her room. I sat down next to him. I got a sideways look and another smile. I reached out my hands and he dove for me, wrapping his arms tightly around my neck as he crawled into my lap. We stayed like that for a long while, me slowly rocking and him resting his head against my chest.

Finally, we stood and, hand in hand, walked out of the room. He stopped to play when he spotted a toy car and I continued on to change my clothes.

But something shifted in those moments. Something deep and powerful clicked inside our hearts with that blazing smile of recognition. This odd couple, this Serbian boy and Midwestern mom, may just be okay, after all.

Author: Tara Lakes

I am a follower of Christ, a wife of twenty years to my best friend, and a mom of eight amazing kids. Seven of my kids were grown in my womb, one was grown in my heart.

SimeonsTrail.blogspot.com

Poverty and Paradise

It's early morning as I relax in my warm home, stretched out in my comfortable, over-sized writing chair, sipping a hot cup of coffee.

My stomach growls and I easily quiet its demands by toasting a bagel. I recognize that the simple act of plugging my toaster into an electric outlet is a luxury not afforded in Haiti. I reflect on the pangs of hunger felt by the children and adults there.

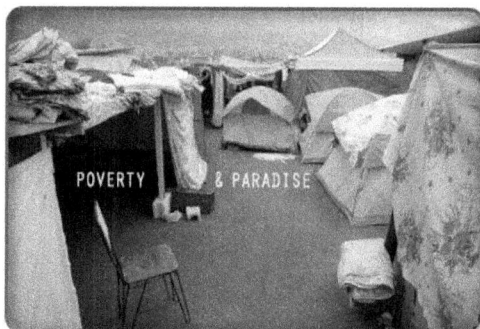

I think about the dry cracked mouths of the children longing to receive something refreshing to quench their thirst. I think about how the beautiful blue ocean taunts them with its rushing waves from their barren tent city. It takes all of the children's strength to walk over to the side of the road. They bend down, resting their dirty, worn clothes on their knees, revealing their calloused, mud-encrusted feet. Feet that walk a journey for which no one would dare ask.

Cupping their tiny hands, they attempt to draw brown-colored water from the ditch on the side of the road. But instead of clear refreshment, they scoop up a bacteria-laden substance and pour it down their parched throats. As it spills onto their hollow cheeks, it also flows into their fragile little bodies, threatening a destructive disease by the name of Cholera.

Preparing to Go

I visited Haiti for the first time in December 2010. I will admit that fear almost choked out my good intentions in traveling to this foreign country. Not only had I recently suffered a stress fracture in my hip, but the deadly disease of Cholera was spreading rapidly throughout Port-Au-Prince and the surrounding villages.

Friends and family lovingly offered advice that leaving the safety and comfort of my home (not to mention my hormonal teenager, vulnerable toddler, and devoted husband) was, to put it nicely, foolish. After all, God gave us wisdom for a reason. There were dangers at every turn. I needed to hear from God.

I decided to shut out the voices around me and "unplug." I fasted from anything that could hinder hearing from God. These included the internet, Facebook, and even TV.

After a few weeks of prayer and silence, I came to my conclusion. I never heard an audible "go," but I deciphered that fear was the only thing holding me back.

The Destination

As we stepped off of the plane and onto the black tarmac I took in the beauty that surrounded me. The sun was setting as we made our way to the warehouse that served as a make-shift airport. As we met eyes with customs officials, I masqueraded as a confident, well-traveled visitor, in an effort to avoid any conflict or obstacles to our mission.

We stepped outside and it immediately resembled more of a Hollywood paparazzi scene than a third-world country. Haitian men clamored about, laying their hands on our bags and feverishly begging in Creole to assist us. I thought about oppression and injustice as I witnessed with my American-bred blue eyes it's obvious consequences.

We hopped on our bus driven by a local, trusted Haitian man. I was thankful for the tinted windows. I felt odd traveling the streets and taking note of their plight. Guilt plagued me, I didn't want to exploit or gawk at them anymore than they already had been.

Tent cities lined the streets by the hundreds, including the median. Fires loomed everywhere. There was no police presence to be found. We traveled through the rubble for three hours until we finally arrived at our location.

Just a few days later I learned the harsh reality of where these children slept at night. While visiting an orphanage I witnessed a young girl sleeping on concrete blocks. She looked so peaceful as the Director explained how grateful he was for those blocks! When it rains, they have no protection from the elements. Floods can easily sweep you away without a moment's notice - a concrete block remains a permanent fixture.

Sacrifice

Throughout the week, as I heard "bonjour" and "bonsai" echo out of these beautiful, charming people, a love began to grow in my heart for them. I thought about the name given to Haiti long ago by the famous discoverer, Columbus. He deemed the island, the "Antilles Jewel" in an attempt to describe its majesty to others. The deep blue sea and the plush green mountains were nothing short of paradise.

And it got me thinking about another place, one mentioned in Genesis. This place was a fruitful garden and our ancestors, Adam and Eve, walked in perfect unity with God and nature there. It too was a paradise that seems but an unattainable luxury.

With this knowledge, I face a dilemma. If God, in my brokenness, didn't give up on me, what right do I have to give up on my impoverished Haitian brothers and sisters? And not only that, but what am I willing to sacrifice in order to help them and their land be restored to its original, serene design?

Several scriptures from God's Word come to mind. Luke 12:28 says, "To whom much has been given, much is required." And James 1:27 says, "Religion that God our Father accepts as pure and faultless is this: to look after orphans and widows in their distress and to keep oneself from being polluted by the world." Mark 10:29 says, "'Truly I tell you,' Jesus replied, 'no one who has left home or brothers or sisters or mother or father or children or fields for me and the gospel will fail to receive a hundred times as much.'"

There is so much searching to be done. To be honest, I'm not sure what this means for me. But one thing I do know is that those sweet faces are forever burned in my heart. I hope that by being willing to obey a calling, I can somehow make their plight a little more bearable - and maybe even beautiful.

Author: Karin Hume

Southern. Mom. Wife. Runner. Writer. Amateur Yogi. Personal Trainer. Contributing writer at Ungrind.org, FreedomUnearthed.com and Allpointswhole.com.

Those Terrorists Over There

Gaza Strip. Arabs. Palestinians. Jews. Hamas. Terrorists. Palestinian Authority. The West Bank. These terms were all jumbled in my head. I didn't get it. The news was confusing. It seemed it was just about "those terrorists over there." I couldn't quite make sense of all the fuss, fear, rockets, air strikes, and tension between Israel and surrounding nations. I wanted to learn and understand, but never thought I'd really figure it out.

I was working in the jungles of Peru when my email account was hacked and I inadvertently started sending out spam emails. Someone responded back. "Umm...looks like you were hacked. Do you want to go on a medical trip to Israel and Gaza with us?" I had been asked three previous times to go, but I had just raised over $5,000 for my mom and I to travel to Peru. I didn't think it was possible... or responsible... or desirable.

Gaza?

You mean the place where I constantly see rocket launchers and people hurling grenades and blood streaming down the faces of protesters? Where those terrorists seem to reside? Where the ladies with Burkas and head coverings live and me-a blonde-haired, blue-eyed American-is likely not welcome?

I had recently finished my Master's Degree in Public Health and

243

gave up my spot in vet school so that I could serve people globally, purposely choosing a life of freelance work to have variety, freedom, and flexibility to say, "Yes" to opportunities like this.

So I said yes.

I said yes because I (thought) I had long ago given up needing every detail to make a decision. I said yes because I had grown tired of saying "no" simply because it was easier…because it was safe.

And then I told my family. They freaked out, naturally. I confidently reassured them that two former Air Force members were coming with us. "What are they going to do?!" they exclaimed. They made a good point. They told me about recent news stories. About their fears and what they saw in the media. I felt like I was throwing caution to the wind. But, I rationalized with them that I could just as easily die in a car accident on the way to the grocery store as die at the hands of a terrorist. Right?

I wondered how I would ever raise another $3,600 to get to the Middle East. So, I unwrapped 600 caramels and baked and sold one-hundred twenty dozen. Fourteen-hundred gooey caramel chocolate chip brownies raised every cent I needed. Money was no longer a barrier.

My team and I hopped on the plane for the Ben Gurion Airport in Tel Aviv, Israel.
Our ultimate goal was to set up a primary health care clinic in The West Bank and then head into the Gaza Strip to work with locals for six days. We were going to set up a clinic in Jibalia, a refugee camp where few if any Americans ever travel.

Plans changed slightly. We were told that we couldn't get into Gaza because of paperwork. "Try back tomorrow," they said.

So we went into Tel Aviv to work at a soup kitchen for a day. We met refugees from Eritrea, Russia, and numerous other countries. We prepared food, handed out clothes, and gave away bags of staple food items. And we learned about the sadness behind their eyes.

The second attempt to get into Gaza. "Try again. Paperwork!"

So, we ran a clinic in The West Bank. Women lined up with their children. Old men sauntered into the clinic to get eyeglasses, blood pressure medication, to be treated for chronic disease. And they smiled. Despite not speaking Arabic, a gentle smile, looking them in the eye, and guiding them back to health professionals was one small way to share reconciliation, love, and compassion. We played soccer with the boys and painted animals and designs on the girls' faces. We handed out toothbrushes and toothpaste, gave massages, and sat and cried with them. And we learned where The West Bank is and met real, live people with stories and hurts and dreams, and in the meantime, saw the humanity behind their veils and head coverings.

The third attempt to get into Gaza. We were told to show up at the The Erez Crossing on the Israeli/Gaza Strip barrier. Men with assault rifles guarded the outside. We waited and each went up to the immigration officer in the booth. I had to give my grandparents' names and answer a slew of questions. They firmly stamped my passport and let me through.

After we reclaimed our luggage, we walked slowly through a maze-like series of passages and then crossed the wall and into

Gaza. After a dusty, hot, mile-long walk, we reached cement barriers and were greeted by several taxis to take us down the road to the checkpoint. In some metal outbuildings, I met members of the Hamas-dressed in dark blue military uniforms-with long, black beards-to have my passport checked. And I learned that we were denied access the first two requests because Hamas' leaders houses were blown up two days before. I was officially in Gaza now. It was surreal to be standing there, letting Hamas members stamp my passport and ask questions.

We were shuttled to our hotel on the Mediterranean. There, we were treated with extreme kindness, curiosity, hospitality, love, and a welcoming, we're-so-glad-you're-our-guests attitude. We ran clinics in Jibalia for three days and met hundreds of people. We saw gaunt horses and donkeys pulling carts. We saw women covered in their hijab. We saw families. We met people who told stories. We prayed with people who had lived through bombings and raids. And we learned about Gaza Strip, Arabs, Palestinians, Jews, Hamas, Terrorists, Palestinian Authority, and The West Bank.

I'm so glad I didn't let fear stop me from meeting people, seeing their humanity, assisting with reconciliation and health care, giving them dignity and honor, and knowing that it's not just "those terrorists over there." I get it now.

Author: Melissa Tenpas

A photographer, world traveler, editor, athlete, adventurer, marketer, dreamer. Community leader working to redeem and love the brokenhearted. Fascinated with God's amazing world. BlondeDutchGirl.com

Reluctant Missionary

As I looked back at the three Indian men saying good bye for the tenth time with tears in their eyes, I was in total awe of what has transpired over the past eight years. I boarded the plane for a 36 hour trip back to the US and thought about the "what ifs", first about me then about them.

I remember the first time I met a man from India; he was here in the US getting his PHD in Theology. As we shook hands he said "some day you will go to India." I thought, no way that's not for me that's for missionaries. I prayed "Father, please don't ask me to go to India. I have nothing to give to them, and beside I do not want to go, end of story."

About 2 years later I was asked to go to India. Not to do mission work, but a business conference. I thought, all right, I can do a business conference. So off I went to India. The agenda was five business seminars, in five different regions, throughout India, in eight days.

During one of the seminars we met people with Campus Crusade for Christ in India. They told us of a training program they were starting to raise up and train young men to plant churches. One of the men on our team said he would share about their project with our home church.

Our church agreed to be part of this project in India, as long as he would lead the new team. He asked me to join him in the project, and I agreed. I can see now that God was helping me take baby steps.

The next trip was scheduled and nine months later I was in India again, this time working with six new church planters. We went into some villages, and some dangerous areas. I witnessed some pretty unbelievable things.

First stop was a small village in the sugar cane country. We met a woman who had been blind since birth. She was now able to see because God had healed her. The people from her house church were all new believers in Christ and had prayed for her healing. She read Scripture to us- Yea God!

The next day we visited a family farm where all twenty-eight family members were new believers. The farm was only about an acre in size and totally supported the family. They lived in two small shelters with no modern day comforts. As we walked around they were harvesting their wheat and grinding their grain. It felt like I had stepped back into Old Testament times.

While we were visiting a young girl, around the age of eleven, approached us. She told us how she had walked over six miles to "meet the white Christian people from the US to pray for her dying little brother." She was the only believer in her family.

When we left the farm we drove by her home, quickly prayed for her brother who was very ill, and tried not to be seen. I don't know what happened to her brother, but I do know that this young believer was grateful and her testimony was greater.

On the long flight back I reflected on how the Lord was changing and preparing me. I now wanted to return to India to be blessed and to see Him at work. But I was not prepared for the next step.

The man that had taken responsibility for getting the program up and running was being transferred to another part of the country. He was leaving a full time lay ministry position open, and someone needed to step up. I said, "that is not me, being a part is one thing, but leader is surely not for me."

Well, four weeks later, with much reservation, I said yes, and committed for only two years. Now 6+ years into this project I am still involved and am working alongside three other lay leaders to oversee what has become a huge program. I cherish the time I spend with the leadership team, now my main focus.

There are over 6,000 new believers, 125 house churches, 17 churches, more than 50 church planters and a new Bible School!

I realized that I had God in a box. I know that God can do anything, as I have seen many times. I know that the Creator of the universe can do anything and He really didn't need me to be the one for His work in India. It may have been different in some ways, but the Lord could have used others to do this work.

So now, by saying yes, I have received many blessing and many accolades that are really about the Father. If I had said no at any time along the journey, that I was too busy, not qualified, or didn't want to do this, if I had not allowed the Lord to help me through these baby steps, I would have missed some of the most meaningful times of my life.

So when you feel called, move forward with full dependence on the Holy Spirit to lead. You too may be in for significant blessing and long term relationship.

A life so different because I made the effort to follow the Spirit.

Author: Jim Burmeister

A husband, a dad, a financial planner, a reluctant missionary, and a son of the Most High.

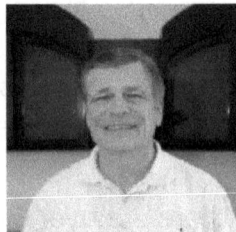

A Moment of Love

There are those moments in life that leave an imprint forever; this is one of them.

My husband and I spent five years living and working in Indonesia. Life there...well, it differed drastically from what we'd always known, and many of those differences were good.

They were differences we embraced.

But there was one... one that was so in-my-face and obvious; wherever we went, there were so many people in need.

In every facet of life, it seemed, there were people hurting...from those with housing needs to being hungry; and others unable to send their children to school or lacking the funds for desperately needed medical care.

And then there were people in the kind of need I'd never seen before.

The first few times it was a shock to see them. We'd stop at a major intersection, and they'd come right up to the motorbike, car, or taxi.

Hands outstretched, eyes pleading, tears brimming.

There were times I had to look away, especially during those first few months. I'd see people who were incredibly thin, crippled to the point of debilitation, even missing limbs.

I'll never forget a certain man, one whose image is printed in my mind and on my heart to this day.

I don't know his name.

My interaction with him was mere seconds.

But that's really all it took to alter my perspective.

There was a part of town we rarely frequented. It was far from both of the houses in which we lived during our time in Indonesia; therefore we would usually find what we needed in a much closer area.

However, this was the true textile part of town, and if we needed craft or jewelry-making supplies or material, there weren't many other places in which to find these things.

So occasionally…maybe two or three times a year, we'd find ourselves in the Asia-Africa part of Bandung.

One Saturday morning I took the bus there with two of my friends. We were on the hunt for some jewelry supplies…and maybe some adventure, too. We spent probably two hours in the area, getting what we needed at a few small shops, before heading back to catch the bus.

The route back to the bus included a walk along a certain stretch of sidewalk where there were a lot of beggars. They would literally set up camp…with perhaps a blanket and a small bag or box containing their worldly possessions.

As we neared the end of the stretch, I noticed a man leaning up against a pillar.

I'm sure I gasped audibly at the sight of him, though I looked only for a second. Whatever had happened to this man was bad… perhaps an explosion or a bad fire. He was horribly scarred.

I quickly looked away and kept walking, feeling an immediate sickness in my stomach.

During the hour-long ride bus ride home, and during the next week, I couldn't shake his image from my mind.

I had known something terrible had happened to him.

I had certainly been aware that he was in need.

And I had done nothing to help, though I could have easily spared a few coins.

It was one of the most convicting moments in my life, a time at which I vowed that I would never again waste such an opportunity to show even a bit of love to another.

The very next weekend I found myself heading to the same area of town with some friends. In fact, I'd be walking that same stretch…and I had this feeling he would be there again.

Sure enough, there he was.

Same pillar.

Same appearance.

Same outstretched hand.

I felt my heart pounding as we approached him.

I prayed... God, give me Your eyes.

Over and over.

I knew I needed to be blind in order to see.

I reached into my pocket and pulled out Rp 10,000. Enough to feed him for the day. It was nothing to me, but maybe everything to him.

I purposely allowed my hand to brush against his as I pressed the bill into his hand and whispered, God bless you. In English, not Indonesian, praying that he somehow understood.

A quiet "terima kasih," (thank you) followed.

And that was it.

I gave that man about (U.S.) $1.00 that day, but what he gave me was so much greater.

A second chance to show the love of Jesus to someone who was in need.

I hope and pray that, wherever he is today, he has found that Love.

Author: Mel Schroeder

Follower of my Father. Wife to Tobin. Mommy to Mae. Friend. Writer. Dreamer. Throw in some coffee, chocolate, running, music...and that's me.

BareFootMel.com

Hitting Hunger Right in The Mustache

I always wanted a mustache. My wife didn't. Not for herself, obviously, but not for me either.

I grew up as a child in the 80's, and my dad was a cop, so for him a mustache and aviator sunglasses were more of an obligation than an option. I remember being 5 or 6 years old and riding in his unmarked Caprice sedan (in the front seat with no seatbelt I'm sure), and turning on the siren to show off to the other kids at little league practice. They thought that was so cool. I did too. Cops were cool, Caprices were cool, and mustaches were definitely cool.

Sometime in the mid 2000s, my obsession with mustaches came back. Long before hipsters were donning them, but shortly after Giambi rocked one to stick it to Steinbrenner. I longed for the rugged good looks of Magnum P.I. , but my wife new better. She new that my aging, balding, pudgy frame would look much more Carl Winslow than Burt Reynolds. She was right. My round face, bald head and thick eyebrows, just made it look like I had three caterpillars starting a seance.

Occasionally I would sneak one in for a Halloween costume or a Tacky Christmas party, but the idea of ever wearing one for more than a few hours was not allowed. Until I got an idea... Sorry, scratch that. Until I stole an idea...

I had heard about some guys in Australia who had started using mustaches to raise money for prostate cancer. Perfect! If I do it for charity, she can't argue that right? Then I started thinking, "If I'm going to do this for a charity, I should make it something that I'm passionate about." It's not like I'm pro-prostate cancer or anything, but it just wasn't something I felt a calling to. So instead I picked an issue that my heart was broken over, world hunger. I presented the idea to my wife, and though she was reluctant, she couldn't say "no" to providing meals to kids who need them. I was in!

The concept was simple: Much like Movember, myself and the few friends I was able to persuade to join would all grow a mustache for the entire month of November. When people noticed something different about us, it would open the opportunity to explain the cause, and solicit their support through financial donations made directly to the charity we were supporting, Feed My Starving Children. We started a blog to track our journey (RightInTheMustache.com), and in the first year we raised over $2,000, which provided over 15,000 meals abroad! My wife never thought that a mustache could actually do good. She was wrong. It was coming back next year.

In 2010, our second year, we set our eyes on doubling the results from year one. Instead, we tripled it! Never underestimate what God can do through a willing vessel, even if that vessel is a mustache.

In 2011 we decided to split our efforts for two causes. We wanted to continue our commitment to providing immediate relief with nutritious meals through Feed My Starving Children, but we also wanted to provide long term restoration through access to clean water with our partner, Blood:Water Mission. We now had two charities to support, and once again, we more than doubled our fundraising to be able to do that.

I'm proud to say that now after 2012 we have raised over $50,000 to fight global poverty, and we have no idea what God will do through us next. What started as an excuse to grow a mustache has changed thousands of lives. Sometimes you not only have to step outside of your comfort zone, but your wife's also. Every year, she cringes on November 1st as the razor approaches my face, and she cries on November 30th when we see the work God has done through us.

In Colossions 3:17 Paul instructs us, "And whatever you do, whether in word or deed, do it all in the name of the Lord Jesus, giving thanks to God the Father through him." Whatever. Whether you bike, or run, or grow mustaches. Do it in His name, and give all thanks and glory to Him. Except for growing a soulpatch. Jesus would never have worn a soulpatch.

Author: Dallas Owen

Every year I organize a fundraiser growing mustaches to provide water in Africa through B:WM. I am thrilled to have another avenue to support them. I love Jesus, my wife, 2 kids and hot chicken.

RightintheMustache.com

A Friendship's Glow

In elementary school we had camp-outs on my parents' back porch. In junior high we taught each other the "bad" words we knew…always writing them down instead of speaking them out loud, of course. In high school we went round and round about college decisions, high school loves, and what our future would be.

We played on the school tennis team together, studied history together, and attempted our art projects together. By senior year we shared a locker…not because we had to but because we figured 'why not?' - we were already sharing everything from a class schedule to our Taco Bell and DQ order that we got for almost every open lunch.

When college came, we went our separate ways.

Our senior year of college we decided to run a half marathon together. I flew down to Glory's school, met her friends, played a little too hard and then ran our half marathon side by side. We both had new, different, lives but our friendship hadn't changed.

Days after graduation I got the call. It was from a good friend, who also happened to be Glory's cousin. He told me Glory was diagnosed with colon cancer, stage 4. We were 21 at the time. I knew my grandpa had cancer, but that was the extent of my knowledge of cancer. We discussed it…"I think there are 5 stages", "it's going to be ok," "she'll get treatment," "she'll be ok"…"right?"

As soon as we hung up, I began frantically searching the Internet in a panic. I immediately realized that everything was far from ok.

The numbers were staring me in the face - they would not go away. Five-year survival rate: 8%.

This is not ok.

I moved out to Denver a couple of months later and had the tremendous honor of being with Glory through her year of treatment. We shared conversations about chemo treatments, doctors, nurses and most of all God. Our friendship became closer than ever before. It was the most authentic, deep, friendship I've ever experienced.

That year was extraordinarily hard, for everyone, but the year was real and full of love. Glory's friends flocked in over the year to visit her. That is what touched me the most. Glory had so many friends, friends of all kinds, from all over, and from all stages of life. So many that visited would say to me, 'Glory is my best friend.' How could one girl have so many best friends?

Glory loved with all her heart. She took care of her friends. She was real with them. I know we will all love deeper because we had Glory in our lives showing us how to love. I'm sure that each and every one of Glory's friends has stories of how they know she loved them. She was truly filled by God's spirit, which allowed her to spill over to everyone she came in contact with. Even those who knew Glory briefly were drawn to her...from the cook at the neighborhood restaurant who encouraged her and made the grilled cheese she craved after chemo sessions, to the nurses and doctors who treated her and are still in touch with her family.

I remember one day in particular when she had received the results from a test that were particularly bad. The cancer was growing rather than shrinking despite all the chemotherapy and radiation. She called and we dived into the results. When our conversation finally paused she said, "Oh my goodness, I haven't even asked you how your day is going, I'm sorry." Really? Glory! There was also the day we brought her home from the hospital for the last time, after the doctors said they couldn't do anything more for her. Despite being so very physically weak, as I helped to get her settled on the couch, and got her oxygen set up, she asked, "Did you get into grad school?" She knew I should have heard that morning. When I said "yes" she used all her breath to say the sweetest softest "Yay!". Glory loved her friends.

They say people either dive in or distance themselves when someone they love is very sick or dying. Being afraid you may lose someone is no reason to pull away. I dove in. I'm not going to lie, it hurts, but I wouldn't change it for the world. I had the honor of being Glory's friend. Glory taught me so much about love, friendship, and faith in God.

Towards the very end of Glory's life, as she fought through the pain and the weakness, God drew her closer and closer to Him. She withdrew from us a bit, but only to be closer to God. I'm comforted to know He was caring for her through everything, and as she got closer to going to be with Him, she was already so close to his presence.

The last thing Glory said to me as we got her situated on the plane, which would take her to a final alternative treatment option, was, "I'll call you when I get there." She passed on shortly after arriving at the treatment center and I never received that call. To say I was heartbroken to learn she wouldn't be making that phone call would be an understatement, but I rest in knowing she will be calling on me when I get to the other side. She will be calling on so many when we get to join her in heaven. We are so incredibly blessed to have had her in our lives on earth. Don't be afraid to dive in, it is worth it.

Author: Becca Marsh

A Kansas girl that would never consider herself a writer but had a story to tell. Currently on a mission to bring the little things in life to young adults affected by cancer.

ProjectGlow.org

Philemon

I've been putting together a trip to New Zealand for awhile... almost 3 years actually. When I was finally nailing down the plans and felt like it was the right time to go, I decided I would throw in a couple days in Fiji on my way there. I had some connections to a hospital project in Fiji, but that didn't end up working out. I was in Africa for a month solid right before my trip, and honestly I had very little time for any planning.

So the bottom line is... I showed up at the airport with absolutely no plan. I talked to some people on the plane on the way there, but that's about it. I arrived in the Nadi airport in Fiji at about 5:30 a.m. Then found the 'local' car rental place, where I was able to bargain a little bit and get a steal on a 4WD vehical. As a photographer I gladly put the money into transportation way before accommodation, as having the right vehicle can get you places for unique shots.

I left the airport in my sweet Hyundai Tucson, focusing more on driving on the left side of the road, than where I was going. After awhile I got my bearing and realized I wanted to go the other way, even though I had no real destination. I turned around, heading toward the bay that I heard on the plane was really pretty.

I drove and drove, finally getting off the main road, and started tearing through dirt trail along the ocean coast. It was beautiful and I was having a blast. I passed through a small village or two and then finally looked ahead and saw a big group of school kids standing around.

It turns out the water was crazier than usual and the tide had come in earlier than expected, creating a sort of water barrier. I pulled up, got out and took some pictures. Afterward I went back to my car and there was an older man there. He looked at me and said "Wow! You look strong!" I shook his hand and said back to him "Jesus makes me strong!" and he said "Praise the LORD!"

We were immediately friends. His name was Philemon.

He was carrying something in a plastic bag but I couldn't really tell what it was. later I realized it was Bible. It turns out God changed his life in 2007 and since then he has been walking from village to village, with mostly idol worshipers or Hindus, sharing the love of Jesus Christ. Philemon was also stuck on that side of water, but had hoped to make it across to visit a certain village that morning. The water was going in and out and I offered to take Philemon across.

I popped it into 4WD and got across no problem. We then went out to the village where we visited huts and shared the Gospel. Philemon later told me that he felt he had faith in God's power, and like Moses, God parted the Red Sea for him and got him across the water in my car. This was a very real statement. He had faith he was supposed to get to the village that morning and through a completely lost, exploring American, God provided that passage.

Mid-morning it started pouring rain, that's when I figured out why he wraps the Bible in the plastic bag. Every morning he walks to villages, every morning it rains, and every morning he carries that Bible, protected inside a worn plastic bag.

After our time in the other villages, he invited me into his home. We went back to his village where his wife and 4 kids were. He knocked down some coconuts from a tree and cut them open with a machete, next thing I knew we were sitting in his bungalow, sipping on coconut milk together.

His wife Sarew made us a fantastic meal and we had a great time together. Interestingly, because of the large Indian settlement years back, our meal was very similar to indigenous food I've eaten while in India, quite tasty.

After lunch, they asked me if I would do them the "honor" of staying with them in their home during my two night stay in Fiji. I decided to take them up on it, and the honor was most definitely mine. I was super blessed by this family and was thankful for how God provided a place for me to stay with a family serving him in Fiji.

Author: Austin Mann

Travel photographer. Facilitator. @WELD.

AustinMann.com

Of Red Sand Beaches and Brown-Eyed Kiddos

We had spent a few hours at the children's home, playing and cuddling and laughing. I was learning a few names and memorizing faces. After dinner was finished Raj, the director of Destiny Children's Home at Impact India, and "Dad" to all the kiddos, packed us all, team and children and staff, up into two vehicles and we drove to the beach.

I hadn't been by the ocean in years and it had never looked as beautiful to me as it did there, in India. The hazy, humid sky was yellow as the sun slipped away through it. The wonderful red sand getting caked onto our shoes. The foamy waves crashing again and again, a never-ending toy for the children to play with.

I had fully intended to hang back from the water. To avoid getting wet and just take in the beauty of where we were. To allow it to sink in that I was finally in India, with children, and to delight in the journey that the Lord had taken me on to get me here. But the children in their excitement were following the waves back out, not seeming to realize that the water was going to come right back up with great force. My motherly heart compelled me to stay close to them, holding their hands so the under-tow wouldn't knock them down, and voice words of warning when the waves began to roll back up to the beach.

Meena had worn her high-heeled sandals down to the water and the tide kept pulling them off. Most times the sandal just sunk into the sand and was easily retrieved, but one time it got pulled away with the receding water. Making sure that the girls stayed far enough back, I scurried after it, catching it up just as another wave crashed on the shore, soaking me up to the knees. The next few waves had a really strong pull as they washed away and Ruthie's footing became unstable. With Meena in one hand, keeping her balanced, I tried to keep Ruthie upright with the other. But she ended up on her rear in the water just as the wave disappeared. Whether out of sadness from being wet or fear from being knocked down, Ruthie returned to the rest of the group crying. How my heart ached to reassure her of her safety.

As I was talking with one of my team mates later, Glory came up to me, lifting her arms up, asking to be held. Remaining fully present in the conversation I was having, but turning my heart toward the little darling, I gladly picked her up and snuggled her. I could tell she was tired. With her head resting on my shoulder and her arm around my neck, her little body grew heavier in my arms the more she relaxed. She never asked to get down, instead she held on tighter as we walked back to the vans. With my soaking wet pants clinging heavily to my legs and my sandals kicking up tons of sand with each step, I was uncomfortable and ready to change into my PJs for the night. Glory was falling asleep in my arms and it felt like she got heavier with each step. Nothing in me wanted to put her down though -- nothing. I scaled the sand dunes with my precious bundle and arrived back at the vans very sweaty and sandy and tired, and oh, so content.

For a girl who doesn't care much for change and gets stressed about the unknown, going to India, where the culture and climate is so opposite of my snug little Midwest life, I should have been uncomfortable and even miserable. And while I was miserable in body, as I went from one physical ailment to the next over the two weeks we were there, I was full of such joy.

I loved waking up with the sun, watching the day become hot and hazy. I loved the cool concrete walls and tile floors of our guest house and the children's home. I loved seeing the faces of children from the washerman community out of our kitchen and balcony widows as they peered in, curious about the white girls inside, and tickled with delight when we smiled or waved at them. I loved walking into the children's home and feeling entirely in-place, not questioning that I belonged right there. I loved giving all my attention to them one at a time -- all my love for them gushing forth in prayers. I loved hearing them cry "Big Sister! Big Sister!" in Telugu over and over. I loved having my heart silently stolen by Glory and Ruthie. I never got it back from them, and I never want to.

I loved the chaotic traffic of those desperate Indian streets, and getting a peek into so many lives as we passed homes and shops and people headed somewhere. I loved every jaw-dropping glance of God's incredible creation. I loved feeling thankful from my head to my toes for every warm, delicious meal that was labored over for us, three times a day. I loved being tired from my head to my toes every night, to the point that even my hard bed with one blanket was truly warm and inviting. I loved every western toilet I encountered like you cannot believe.

I loved the dirt that got on my shoes and clothes as I sat in the slums with children who spoke with me even though we didn't understand one another. I love that even now my flip flops are coated in red sand from our trip to the beach with the children. That is where I left a portion of my heart, and that is where it will stay -- there on the red sand beaches of Visakhapatnam, India with those little brown-eyed kiddos.

Author: Chelsea Mills

Chelsea, a twenty year old blogger from Wisconsin, is compelled by the sacrificial love of her Lord to advocate for vulnerable children and to love her neighbors, at home and abroad.

YourReasonableService.blogspot.com

Beautiful Haunting

Sometimes the gospel smacks you up side the head. I'm glad of that.

Fall, a year and a half ago, was a particularly restless time for my soul. So I prayed, "God, show me your heart. What do you love, what moves you?" And he did.

In no time my life was overflowing with the truth of adoption. God, the great adopter, was leaning in and inviting me to understand the gospel in a whole new way. My inbox, devotions, conversations all seemed to scream the same truth. God loves the brokenhearted, offers them a home, and invites his adopted children to do the same.

I was hooked and started pursuing this truth like a treasure hunter. One night as I sought God's next steps I 'stumbled' upon a video. It was produced six years ago by Ann Curry. The footage was taken in the fetid confines of several Serbian mental institutions. There were sights that would break your heart and bring a strong man to his knees. Over the next week I watched and re-watched the video, haunted by the pain, compelled to respond.

One night as my computer replayed the terrible footage of broken humanity, I paused the documentary, fixed on the image of a young boy. Or was he a man? His emaciated, bent body was crammed in a crib. He couldn't speak, feed himself, or even roll over. The bars were his world. But I saw something in his eyes. As his face was touched his eyes flickered emotion, longing, humanity.

Tears streamed down my face. Reaching out my fingers I stroked his image and prayed. "God, just let me touch him. I need to touch these people. I need to know the truth. I'll go, send me."

Over the next weeks I stumbled my way towards Serbia. The documentary I had watched was years old and I knew Serbian laws and society were changing. Did people still live like this? I called my church's denominational leaders, missions boards, searched online for updated information about these institutions, but found little help or answers.

I did come in contact with a human rights organization in Serbia and asked them for their input and help. They gave me the email address of a mental institution in Novi Sad, Serbia. I emailed the director and asked if I could visit. He said yes.

Within weeks I was on a plane with a dear friend. Through the amazing support of friends, family, and even strangers God had provided the money, and then some, to visit for a week. My stomach was in knots as love blazed a trail. What would we find? How would we be received?

What I found at the institution was friends. Six hundred residents and not enough hands or money to care for them all, but creativity and love shined nonetheless. The circumstances challenging and painful, but the conditions not as severe as I had expected.

The young man in the video, who had originally propelled me forward, wasn't in this institution, but his brothers and sisters in suffering were.

In a white, metal crib, much like the ones I had seen in the video, I found another little boy who has compelled me to continue to speak and pray and return.

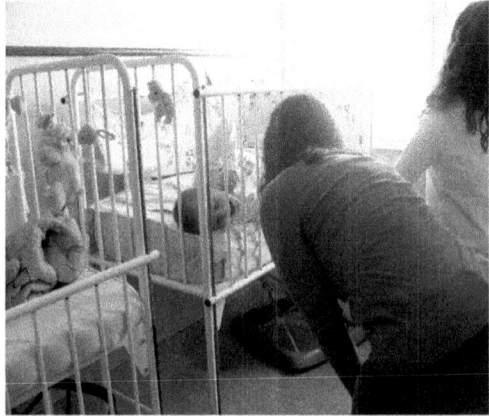

For a while on a warm, October afternoon, in a world far from my own, I held the hand of a little boy with blonde hair, blue sparkly eyes, stick legs, and a mind damaged by meningitis. His sweet hands were rough and dry, calloused from being chewed. A habit induced by boredom. He smiled and chuckled and held on tight as I sang to him.

At the end of the day a realization swept over me, it was Jesus' hand I had been holding.

I may not have followed the traditional path of adoption I originally set out on. And I may never be privileged to adopt one of those precious children with disability. But I have adopted them as my responsibility, I've adopted their needs as my own, I've adopted their lives into mine.

Life is teaching me that sometimes adopting a person into your family doesn't look like bringing them home to live. Sometimes it means joining them where they are and drawing them into God's family with our very presence.

Dictionary.com defines adoption as a verb, meaning: to choose or take as one's own; make one's own by selection or assent.

There's an entire world waiting to be adopted.

Author: Beck Gambill

Following Jesus all the way home. I write about the journey, people that inspire, and beauty all around. I'm looking for mercy at every turn.

BeckGambill.wordpress.com

Martini Explorers

There's a vacation and then there's a journey. Make no mistake; Machu Picchu is not a vacation. You certainly can do it in luxury lodges, on vista trains and with DLSR cameras, but that's not the Incan experience and it's a far cry from your couch and the remote (well, remote in a very different kind of way).

It's a trip for martini explorers (Mark Adams, "Turn Right at Machu Picchu"). For people who are accustomed to a certain degree of luxury, but who suffer from an undeniable restlessness to see the world. It requires a full immersion of mind, body, and soul. And unless you are ready to make that commitment, you will be disappointed.

I however, was not.

I can better explain what the Inca Trail isn't than what it is. It's definitely not your first trip across the pond to marvel at ancient sites. It's also not backpacking because you're not roughing it. It's a pilgrimage trip.

It is also not a walk in the park. It's simultaneously the longest and shortest four days of your life. You will come back more exhausted and disheveled than you left. No sane person would trade a week of umbrella drinks for roughing it sans showers, buy your own toilet paper and 11 hours of exercise a day. But it's so much more than that.

The Trip

I am not what you call super in shape. When I first booked our trek three months out I thought I had plenty of time to prepare. And I did put in solid gym hours for the first few weeks, but then the holidays came and you can fill in your own excuse here. I knew it would be the hardest thing I'd ever do physically, but it was all about attitude. It would be 100% mind over matter. If people can run 26.2 mile marathons in a matter of hours, surely we could conquer the same distance over a span of four days.

At our pre-hike meeting we learned that our crew would include 15 Americans, two guides and 22 porters, also known as the Red Army. Llama Path, our chosen guides, called themselves the super hiker group. TripAdvisor research fail. To give you some perspective, the Inca trail actually starts at about 9,000 feet and ends even lower than that at approximately 8,000 feet. A common misconception is that you're climbing up to Machu Picchu. In reality, you're tackling two massive passes at 14,000 feet and 13,000 feet, going back down to 11,000 in between and then finally descending on the Sacred Valley.

With only two peaks to scale, where our group stopped for lunch the second day is where every other group sets up camp for the night. We however, would be doing both obstacles at once so we could "take it easy the third and fourth days" (aka only six hours of hiking). I knew day two would be brutal, especially with the highest point ominously named "Dead Woman's Pass."

Day one was six hours of "flat" terrain. Now, flat in Incan is really an inside joke to mess with the Gringos. It meant jagged stones and alternating inclines/declines. I was actually leading the pack, making small talk with the main guide, Castiano (who, bless his heart, I will never forget that his name translates to "almost anus").

Then we started going uphill. My body seemed to forget that I used to live in Colorado because I could not for the life of me catch my breath. It wasn't altitude sickness because I wasn't dizzy, nauseous, or getting headaches, I just literally could not stop hyperventilating. It was frustrating because I wasn't sore or tired; I just knew I needed to slow down for fear I was going to have a heart attack at age 28. I struggled to camp and was welcomed with snacks and coca tea. (Which for the record is a legal version of cocaine, "Incan Red Bull," not chocolate like I innocently assumed). Running through my mind was one down, three to go. Day two would be the real challenge.

And it was. Four grueling hours straight upstairs. I could not breathe. I was forced to take breaks every few steps and didn't see anyone for most of the day. So far behind, I had my own guide to make sure I didn't collapse.

Make no mistake; going downhill is equally as challenging, but for different reasons. At that altitude is the cloud forest, which brings spells of pelting rain, causing the ground to give out and become a mudslide. You are literally bracing yourself so as not to lose your footing and slide downhill. And as much as you buy the newest quick-dry gear, it's no match for how frequently the weather changes, alternating from boiling to soggy in a matter of minutes.

After the sheer exhaustion of getting 2-4 hours of sleep, feeling like a drowned rat and being pushed to the physical limit, I hit my wall and started bawling uncontrollably. I begged the guides to let me stop and continue on in the morning. Obviously this was not an option. Most areas are so remote that helicopters are not even allowed. If something serious were to happen, one of the porters has to take you the rest of the way on piggyback.

We're talking men who are between 18-50, barely 5'5, already carrying 60 lbs. while wearing flip flops because they can do the entire run in four hours. I wasn't about to deal with that embarrassment.

I was taking so long though that the last hour was spent descending in the pouring rain and pitch black. Gustavo, who had become my personal guide, had to hold my hand so I wouldn't fall flat on my face. It felt like the blind leading the blind.

After hearing "only twenty minutes more" 45x, I zoned out. Day three and four were a blur. All I can remember about Machu Picchu itself is it really does come out of nowhere. It feels like you're walking, walking, walking with no end in sight, and then bam, out of the clouds it rises like a Phoenix. Those wily Incans.

The Aftermath

With my ADD on overdrive during the history lessons, the sheer magnitude of where we were, what we had accomplished, and what we saw didn't hit me until the flight home.

People speed through the trail to find the mirage of a hidden civilization at the end, but the real wonder is in getting there. You are walking the same path as millions before you. The Inca Trail is four days to imagine life as it was, disconnect, and erase all traces of modern society.

It forces you to stop, slow down, and appreciate the flora and fauna. Endless peaks, mystical cloud cover, bridges to nowhere, stairs through time. It is undeniably the edge of the earth.

Very few trips inspire such self-reflection. Peru as a country was highly underwhelming. Lima was overcast, gloomy, and sorely run down with casinos and KFC's on every corner. The experience was one for the record books, though. Everyone had their own challenges. Some had stomach bugs, some had bad knees, but we all pushed through.

I challenge you to go find your own inspiration. If you happen to do the hike, the most practical piece of advice I can give is to do squats instead of the stairmaster (you'll thank me when it comes time for those holes...).

Just remember to breathe. And get off your couch!

Author: Lauren Monitz

An avid foodie/travel lover and lifestyle writer hailing from Chicago, Lauren has a master's in E-business, six years of Online Marketing experience, and an endless supply of sassy, random stories.

LaurenMonitz.com

Laying It Down

I sit in the metal chair, trembling, seeing the images of the past, static, but deathly real, black-and-white heavy on a pulled down screen.

The room is full, some faces I know, many I don't. I am still afraid, ashamed. Again, I hardly believe what I have done.

The kind woman on the platform shares about her organization who counsels and gives women with unintended pregnancies support--His support--and her words penetrate. The room is dimmed for the photos on the screen: the waiting room, the counselor's office. I know those places, and the room spins. Who was that girl? My heart pounds.

The memory of not choosing You and the cost, the cost it has had on my heart.

"Let it go, again, child. Tell them, say it again, for you know now I am here."

I have come to this room to give a simple announcement, to let this room full of mothers know about an opportunity to serve moms--most needy, I say--who struggle financially to be able to keep their babies.

Most needy. But this isn't conditional, a situation of finances, is it? To be in that place of most need: aren't we all?

My desperation for God makes me reel, flattens me so I doubt I can stand, let alone speak. I am convinced it would be better for my dear friend who sits beside me, holding me up with His love without knowing it - to make the announcement for me. But my beating heart tells me this is for me.

I am through with not choosing You, Father.

I see He has brought me here, not just to make an announcement about a project these women can hear about in a church bulletin. He has brought me here to redeem me again.

Twenty-two years, Father, and You still teach me what it is I need to let go. Keep me here then. Help me not reject You again. Help me not be that girl.

I sit frozen to my chair, remembering my past decision to have an abortion, at sixteen years old, my former dead heart without Christ in it. I am that girl, in the orchard night, writhing, believing death has come--all from the mere threat of the world knowing her sin of having sex before marriage. I am the girl who couldn't bear family and friends knowing she messed up. I am the girl who couldn't imagine throwing away all she had worked so hard for-trading the life of a baby not mine to give up, for the selfishness of a girl believing the lie that death is better than truth. I am the girl who believed holding on to pride, my dead life, looked better than anyone knowing the darkness of my sin.

My pride: how could I think to give that up?

Oh, God. What are You stirring in me again?

"I no longer want death. I am not living there anymore."

Listening to this dear woman speak about helping girls like me, I want so badly to run again. But this time, I don't. For that is no longer what I do: run.

I have received the new heart I prayed for, despaired for--the heart longing for Life. I am not that girl anymore. But I need to stay close to her, comfort her, continue to fight for her heart with His truth and light in me. I can no longer run from moments that give me the chance to confess that I am saved from death, from the death the heart of that girl brings. I have to continue to let go of my pride and hold fast to His truth now. I am tired of running.

You have fought for my heart, Father, and now, I am not letting it go.

I rise when it is my turn to speak, tears wiped away, hands shaking. What comes out of my mouth isn't the clean, safe announcement I had planned. But it was about that girl then, and about the redemption in me now. And it was true.

I am grateful for the opportunities He gives me to choose Him and proclaim His life in me. And that is where I want to stay, in this place of letting go of my pride.

And although I am full of sorrow for the choice I made those years ago, I am grateful for His life, His salvation, as He has shown me the depths of the darkness of my heart. I know who that girl is without Him.

Keep me humble, Father. You came for that girl. You come for her still to remind me, while I am not that girl with the dead heart anymore, to stay with You, to stay Alive, I need to continue to lay pride down.

Almighty, Father, come.

Author: Jennifer Camp

Voice finder; wife of heart-warrior; mom of three; encourager of My Girls; God searcher; outdoor lover; womens' heart pursuer: my desire to live in my true identity, in God's eyes.

YouAreMyGirls.com

A Couch Dream

I like my couch. Mine is grey, but I call it 'silver' to be cool. It is huge, with a giant chaise, which means there is plenty of room when watching a game. I have a coffee table, which is great for entertaining and getting crumbs on. Below that is a rug, brown and shaggy. To be honest it really makes my couch feel more homey and cozy--it ties in the room. My couch is the central point in my living room. I sit there, eat there, talk there, make important phone calls there, and conduct one of my most important activities there: watching football.

If I could choose, I would want a couch in every room, even the kitchen. I wish there were a built-in toilet, or bathroom mechanism so then I would never-truly have to leave it. My ideal couch would have a coffee machine, and a miniature fryer to cook chicken wings and french fries. There would be a fountain of sorts that spewed Dr. Pepper or possibly a nice refreshing Gatorade drink. There would be a button that I could press and my wife would come rushing in to massage my feet. And there would be a space for showering that was positioned just right so it wouldn't hinder my view of the television.

It is my couch that makes my home truly a home--or so I thought. Eighteen days after May first, a little boy was born, a boy that would claim the name Mozzie Anthony Beaverson, and with that event my definition of a home would change.

I was thin. Limber. Long haired, and I could barely grow a mustache. Okay, I wasn't even close to growing a mustache. I was twenty-one but didn't look a day over eighteen. My wife sat in our couch as we discussed making a life-changing decision.

"We are so young, it seems ridiculous!" My wife said.

"I know, we are barely bringing in a paycheck" I replied, as we seemingly agreed and discussed the phone call that could change our life. There was a girl who was pregnant, who, for some reason, asked my wife and I to adopt her little boy.

Something deep down in my belly, you know the area deep down in that part of your body that you didn't even know existed, well that part was somehow telling me that it was right. It seemed so silly, yet so clear. And my wife somehow felt the same way. As we sat in a tiny studio apartment we decided that adopting a little boy was suddenly going to become a reality.

My wife worked hard, probably too hard. I studied full-time at college and worked 30 hours at a theater, and still interned at a local church. Life was hard enough. The feeling of coming home, sitting on my couch and putting my feet up, was heaven to me.

Despite my love for that couch...my wife and I decided to go. We left to get our son.

He was born before I turned twenty-two. I had officially adopted a child. It seemed surreal. I sat in the NICU and slept in a chair somehow trying to wrap my mind around the fact that my son was here. Parents typically have nine-months to prepare for their child, we only had seven. And these seven months were filled with paperwork, home studies, and constant battles between people's words of "you shouldn't" or "you're making the wrong decision."

The crowd would say to stay at home, to do it the right way, and they would say that the odds were against us. They seemed right. I mean why would we do this? It was not our plan, it was not our parents plan.

But maybe it was somebody else's plan.

So today, as my wife and I sit in our tiny apartment on our grey couch...I hold a baby. Or at least try to--he loves to play. My "couch dream" suddenly is lost. My life is better than my couch could offer me. If it were not for our decision to get up from that couch and leave this comfortable place, then maybe I would still be sitting there. But I do know that my home, which was defined by my couch, is now defined by the little dude who snoozes in a tiny bed just down the hall.

As we hold him, he holds us. He is small, but in our arms he seems so big. I'm twenty-three, my wife not much older. But our life is now defined by an adventure, an incredible story that we can now share, and an incredible family to share it with, and an incredible God who stood beside us every step of the way.

I'm a couch rebel. One who prays that my son will not defined by his couch, but by his ability to get up off of it.

Author: Alex Beaverson

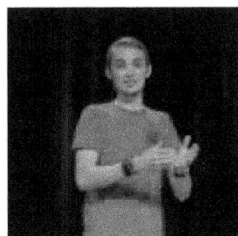

Skinny White Male. Director at Mariners Church High School Ministry. Husband. Father. Speaker. Writer. Thinker. Blogger.

SkinnierThanAverage.com

Hope is Always a Miracle

In the early winter of 2004, amidst ordinary days, my life changed forever. One night a friend invited me to join a group of people for dinner, and mentioned that a friend of his was visiting from out of town. Since I had no plans I accepted the invitation.

And I met the man that I thought I would marry.

He was handsome, funny, and most importantly shared my faith. Over the course of five days I developed a crush and although we lived thousands of miles apart, our futures, which had been planned before we met each other, were about to connect in England.

But the future did not end in the way my heart had dreamed and less than a year later nothing was the way I had planned. First, due to financial reasons I did not move to England. Second, I was heartbroken as the guy was no longer in the picture. Third, a persisting pain in my right side was growing worse every day. I saw several doctors and was assured by all that stress was the source of the pain. While I wanted to believe them I had a nagging feeling that something was terribly wrong.

Unfortunately I was right.

One day I was sitting on the couch when suddenly I felt like the insides of my body exploded. I was rushed to the emergency room where the doctors found that I had ten cysts simultaneously burst. I was told by the doctors that since these cysts had been the cause of the daily pain that I would now be fine.

By May it became obvious that I was not "fine" and once again ended up at the emergency room where I was informed that I would have to have emergency surgery. The doctors had found a large mass the size of a football covering my right ovary. Due to the size the doctors warned me that I probably had an aggressive form of Ovarian cancer. One doctor mentioned that it might be a good time to start praying for a miracle.

At twenty-five I thought I might die.

But instead of cancer they found that the large mass was Stage IV advanced Endometriosis. After the surgery my doctors' first words were: "The good news is it's not cancer but welcome to a life of pain."

I obtained additional doctors' opinions but all agreed with his grave words. The consensus was that since I had such a severe case I had little hope of living a pain free life. The only suggestion was to try a treatment of prescription drugs.

It quickly became obvious by August that none of the treatments that typically work for most women were going to work for me. I consulted with several additional doctors from around the world and was prescribed stronger drugs. After several weeks it became obvious that these too were not going to help and I was having a difficult time with the side effects which included vomiting, my hair turning white or falling out, and losing some of my memory. By the end of August it was impossible to move out of my bed because the pain was so great. I didn't want to believe it, but it appeared that the original doctor had been right.

My life at twenty-five was wasting away in a bed with no hope of change. I contemplated suicide as I did not see an end in sight to the pain. I didn't because Psalm 18:6 and 46 came to my mind every time I thought about ending my life. The Lord's quiet still voice and presence met me right where I was and became my closest companion. My prayers changed from begging to be healed to begging the Lord to be merciful.

In September, under the care of a new doctor, I agreed to another surgery. In October, I flew across the country with my mom and had surgery. The predicted one hour surgery ended up lasting several hours. The disease had spread so aggressively that parts of my organs had to be removed. I was the worse patient that he had seen of my age group and because of the severity I ended up in several medical journals.

After months of recovery I finally started to live a normal life one pain-free day at a time. Many doctors from around the United States that said my case was a miracle and stated that it must have been "something higher" that had healed me. It truly was a miracle. It will be eight years in October 2013 and I am so thankful to share that I have had no additional surgeries, drugs, pain, or endometriosis problems.

It is a miracle.

People ask me if I think God "finally" showed up. My answer is always "no". The truth is God was present the entire time even during my darkest days and nights. He hears our prayers and holds all of our tears.

I do not assume that everything works out happily on this earth. I, along with many others, could share stories of pain that do not have a "miracle" ending. Over the course of these eight years, I have experienced heartbr. My ex-fiancé' walked away from our relationship and just this spring I have been diagnosed with three health issues, including advanced late stage chronic Lymes disease and cancer that have not been healed yet.

Maybe it is not always about the miracle we think we are looking for.

Maybe we don't always have answers or miracles, but we do always have hope. And maybe the hope we dream of is not the answer we wanted. Maybe it is just the hope of realizing that when all the dreams are shattered a new dream is just beginning.

And that type of hope is always a miracle.

Author: Rebecca VanDeMark

I am a writer, teacher, speaker, and blogger who loves Jesus, life, the concept of hope, and all things pretty as I survive and thrive with advanced late stage lymes disease and cancer.

Caravansonnect.com

Rising from the Ashes

November 3, 2008, and June 10, 2011, are two days that are indelibly engraved in my memory. On each of those days, I heard words that chilled me to the bone: Your house is on fire. I wasn't home when Aaron called me with the news: I was in WalMart buying chocolate candy, marshmallows, and graham crackers for s'mores, and hot dogs and buns so he and his friends could have a cookout that night. I never expected that I would be the one to leave a loaded buggy in the middle of WalMart, race to the car, and drive home at speeds that would normally require clearance from air-traffic controllers. I drove down the powerline right-of-way to see my front yard filled with ambulance and rescue squad trucks, fire trucks, and sheriff's deputies cars. After the sheriff, the next person I saw was Corey, a young man I had taught in Sunday school and had watched grow up.

"What are we going to do?" I wept into his shoulder.

"You're going to be okay," he said. "God's got you."

That evening and night, neighbors came by. Someone gave her coat to hold off the autumn chill. Corey's mother, who had just buried her older son, brought fried chicken and the trimmings for our supper to be eaten later at my parents' home, where we would live for the next six months. Other neighbors and strangers contributed money so that the next day I could go out and buy the necessities--clothing for us all, toiletries, groceries. Friends and family offered their help.

Yes, we were going to be okay; God did have us. We were able to build a new home, and seven months later, we moved in. Life was good. We were recovering.

Until June 10, 2011, when those words hit again: Your garage is on fire. I've called 911. This time, I had to face the dragon alone. I tried not once, but twice to turn on the water hose to cool down the side of the house next to the fire. The flames were incredibly hot on that 99-degree summer afternoon. I was so helpless, so frightened, so defeated. It was my neighbor who took me away from the flames and discovered that I had second and third degree burns to my right arm and right cheek. I felt no pain then.

At that point, I couldn't think of anything except, "I can't do this again."

But again, God had me and my family in the palm of His strong hands; He held me next to his shoulder where I wept, "What are we going to do?" He is the one who said, "You will be okay; I've got you."

Over the next six months, we lived with my parents again; we purchased a much smaller single-wide mobile home, and moved back to our home of the last 27 years. I was unemployed still, having left my teaching job of 22 years. I wasn't certain how we would make it through these hard times. There were days of despair and depression, days of weeping. But through it all, God had us in the palm of His hands.

Today, two years after the second fire, I come to the couch next to the window where I can watch the birds gather at the feeders. I watch them flit in and away; I listen to them sing and chirp without worry about where the next seed will come from. I draw strength from them, trusting in Jesus's words to his disciples. If God provides for the birds of the air and clothes the lilies of the field, how much more will He provide for me, His daughter.

I have healed from the burns, thanks to my neighbor's quick response with ice packs and immediate first aid and to the medical team at the Steele Burn Center in Augusta, Georgia, where I went for treatment throughout the summer, fall, and winter of 2011 and 2012. God does provide for our needs, and He does make miracles. I still have not found employment, but I have used my time at home to grow closer to God. I have led some incredible women in a private Facebook group for empty-nest moms, and I have participated in a God-sized Dream Team with more incredible women who love the Lord.

In a funeral service, the pastor says that we move through the cycle of "ashes to ashes and dust to dust." I am rising from the ashes, much like the phoenix of mythology, to become a new creation. It took literal ashes to make that resurrection happen.

Today, I wait patiently for a phone call, one that I pray will return me to a classroom. I am trusting God to lead me along the path that will bring Him the glory. I am not only rising from ashes, but I am redeemed.

Author: Olivia Fulmer

I am a mom to two grown boys, ages 24 and 20; a wife of 29 years to Grady. I am a retired high school English teacher. But most important, I am a daughter of the Almighty Father God.

OneWordThisYear.wordpress.com

Finding Family

Family.

After traveling to Cambodia to visit some dear friends, Eric and Ginny Hanson, family is what I found. Eric and Ginny are the founders of In His Steps International, a non-profit ministry based out of Phnom Penh, Cambodia. I specifically traveled with a team to Cambodia to work with Sak Saum, an arm of In His Steps which works with women who are in danger of, or have been victims of human trafficking. Sak Saum means "dignity" in Khmer, the Cambodian language. Ginny started Sak Saum and her desire is to see exploited women find freedom, purpose, healing and love in their own lives and in the lives of their families.

I was privileged to meet and work with all of the Sak Saum girls during my stay in Cambodia. Our arrival was met with a beautiful dance, in which we were showered with flowers, that are still pressed and tucked safely away in my favorite book! Each girl was so different, and yet each had beautiful qualities about her – a gentle smile, a shy glance my way, an outgoing and rambunctious personality! I found that it was hard for me to not be able to communicate with them because of the language barrier, and although I loved every minute of being with them, that night I went back to our team house frustrated. I remember the first evening laying in the dark and waiting for sleep to come, and all I could think about was how much I desired to just sit with each girl over coffee and share our stories, our dreams, passions and desires. I began to think about how I could communicate my deep desire to be friends with each one and fell asleep praying and thinking about it.

When we returned the next day, I decided to just sit with the girls while they worked. Conversations went on around me that I didn't understand, but they began to pull me into the conversation by asking me little questions. As I answered them we began to question each other on words we didn't understand, and to teach each other as we went. That day as I left, my journal was filled with my written version of Khmer words paired with pictures so I could remember them, and my heart was full as I remembered our time laughing at each other as they learned English and I tried to learn Khmer. In the next days I began to feel a strong kinship for each of the beautiful girls that were there. They welcomed me and each one of the team with open arms – always open to trying new conversations, sharing their food with us, and showing us genuine love.

On one of the evenings we were there, we took a trip with our team into town. While riding in the tuk tuks, I knew something was terribly wrong with my stomach! All the way into town I was willing myself to not be sick, and hoping that I would magically feel better. When we arrived we set up an area next to the waterfront where we prepared to eat a picnic dinner and enjoy the surrounding city life. Before I knew it, my sickness had come to its peak and I raced to the side to lose everything within me...but right behind me rushed up one of my sweet Cambodian sisters, to hold my hair back and rub my back. I'd known these girls for a few days, and that night each one of them showed their concern, and doted on me like a loving sister. I felt loved and valued. The very thing I wanted to communicate to each of them, they were pouring into me.

One of the women I specifically connected with is Sana, a young woman full of spunk and fun. Sana knew she did not want to follow in the unfortunate footsteps of her great grandmother, grandma, and mother, so she entered Sak Saum for the training and hope it provided. I could always count on Sana to play tricks on me while I was there, teasing me and giggling every time I fell for them. Every time we worked with Sak Saum, Sana and I would seek each other out, sit next to each other and attempt conversation, laughing every time we misunderstood. On our final day in Saang, Sana stayed by my side until we had to leave. We hugged each other and cried as we said goodbye, waving tearfully as our van drove off. She called me Sister before I left, and I knew that I'd found a "forever family" right there in Cambodia.

Sana has a feisty and strong spirit, and has weathered many storms in her life, but she chooses joy, happiness and love. She has been given the chance at a life that the rest of the women in her family never had, and I know that she prepares the way for freedom for generations to come. Sana is married now and learning to be a wife, while taking care of her mother-in-law. Even now, three years later, each message I receive from her makes me long to be back in Cambodia.

We believe when we travel to another country that we will change the lives of those we meet, but instead we find ourselves changed. Something special happened while in Cambodia, I gained something that I didn't even know I was missing – I found family, friends and sisters, not by blood, but in the depths of my heart. I left a piece of my heart in Cambodia the day I left, and although that is painful, I wouldn't change a thing about it.

So, get up off the couch, and go be a couch rebel, but don't go thinking you will change others, go expecting to be changed.

Author: Jeni Mason

Jeni is passionate about relationships, mentoring others and seeing people thrive both in the United States and abroad. Jeni is new to the blogging world but is excited to be a part of it!

WillNotBeSilentBlog.wordpress.com

Feeding 1,000

Have you ever witnessed a miracle?

I have.

In December 2007 I was in Pacalsdorp, South Africa, with a ministry called Camp South Africa. Our missions team was set to visit a local church and host a day camp for local children. We were told to expect around 400 people. When we arrived early that morning to set up, approximately 400 people had already assembled and we could see people continuing to flood into the churchyard from the local squatter camp. More and more children came, followed by moms and dads, grandpas and grandmas.

People had heard we were coming, and they wanted to see for themselves. We were prepared with a program of games, music, the Gospel presentation, and food for our guests. We were delighted to see so many people, but as the minutes passed we started to get worried; how were we to feed so many people? We had enough sandwiches to feed 400 people, but the numbers were quickly growing. As the team started to organize games, our numbers continued to grow. Each team member was creating games on the spot to accommodate nearly 50 people each. It was mind blowing! We had no idea how many people were there.

During the presentation of the Gospel, we were able to get an estimated headcount. We had nearly 1,000 men, women, and children in attendance! Yes, 1,000.

We praised God for bringing this many people to hear His Truth.

We praised God for the opportunity to share His love. But how were we to feed them? How would our 400 sandwiches feed 1,000?

We prayed. And prayed. And prayed.

As we wrapped up the Gospel presentation, the women and children were sent around the building to a window located in the kitchen. We were going to hand a sandwich, a bag of chips, and a juice to each guest through the window. My teammate and I stood outside the window to help organize the crowd. As the people flooded around the building, I could see that organization was going to be difficult; no, scratch that, it was going to be impossible.

Very quickly we were completely surrounded. Teenagers and children were being pushed forward by their mothers. Moms were holding up their babies screaming "give my child food" in Afrikaans. People were getting pushy. People were getting angry. Men were trying to sneak in to steal food from the children. Teenagers were pushing the little ones out of the way. Elbows were flying, hurtful words being yelled, an angry crowd was upon us.

I was overwhelmed.

I was getting squished against the building.

Anxiety was setting in.

My directions were being ignored.

It was hot, it was sticky.

It was as if everything was in slow motion.

The looks in their eyes.

The hunger they were experiencing.

I saw it all, in slow motion.

My teammates in the kitchen kept whispering into my ear, "we're almost out", "we only have about 20 more sandwiches", "What should we do?". "Pray" I responded, "keep praying". While a few of us manned the window and the serving of guests, the rest of the team was inside the church praying. Praying for enough to feed all. Praying that we'd have enough food to feed the 1,000.

I don't really know how to explain what happened. I am still speechless at the thought of that day.

Tears still well up in my eyes.

Somehow we had enough.

Our prayers were answered.

Everyone ate.

Every single one of those men, women, and children got food and we had a few sandwiches to spare.

We fed them all.

He fed them all.

I remember walking around the churchyard after the chaos had died down. I watched as hungry children devoured their sandwiches. I watched as teenagers fed their little brother or sister and stuck the chips in their pockets for later. I witnessed Moms giving their sandwich to their child. The emotions I felt were almost overwhelming. As tears streamed down my cheeks I just kept walking in circles around the church yard. I could hear my heavy breathe reverberate throughout my body. I had just witnessed the most amazing miracle. God provided. God provided in a BIG way.

God took sandwiches for 400 and fed 1,000.

I vowed to never forget. I vowed to never forget this miracle; His miracle.

I witnessed what the disciples had witnessed. I saw Him take seven loaves and a few fish (Matthew 15) and feed 1,000. I saw Him multiply what little we had to care for a thousand. I witnessed a miracle and I vowed to never forget that He provides. He always provides.

So why do I have such a hard time remembering that? Why am I so forgetful?

Why do I worry that He will provide?

He will provide, He has promised us that.

"And my God will supply all your needs according to His riches in glory in Christ Jesus. Now to our God and Father be the glory forever and ever. Amen."- Philippians 4:19

Are you praying for a miracle? Keep praying.

Do you have a need? Keep praying.

Have you lost hope? Keep praying.

Because my God, our God, will supply all your needs. He has promised us that.

Let us draw near to the King and be filled with hope.

Author: Mandy Scarr

Writer. Reflector. Lover of all things beautiful. Wife. Soon-to-be Mom. Encourager. Peanut-butter addict. Speaker. Dreamer. Life-giving community lover.

MandyScarr.com

Travel Bug

In the course of a week, I have been called Amish, hip (hipster), and "off the chain." All this week, all while on the job.

Not unfamiliar to culture and cultural differences, at least some of the time, I had to laugh at how different the comments were. I don't necessarily see myself as any one of these things; however, interesting environments call for interesting lingo and commentary.

Much of my life is spent putting out fires (not literally, I don't like fire). My job is to go into people's homes, not just people who you see with smiles plastered on their face all the time, but whose day-to-day is very real, and who know what it is to have to overcome challenges. I've been a counselor for young kids and teens for a couple years now, and have spent most of my years working with youth in some capacity.

I struggle to write about my role in kids' lives now. Part of it is that I'm limited in some ways. If I could, I'd talk all day about my kids and their stories of bravery, about how they are special and unique, about what it is to be strong.

I want to place light on the area that God has put me to counsel right now, so I search for ways to highlight this love, to create words for what's complicated.

When I test the waters with people, try to explain what I do, what I'm passionate about, it raises eyebrows sometimes, or causes many questions. That's okay. Maybe you do that with your job.

Do you ever want to tell people you are an entrepreneur sometimes, or something else, like working for the circus?

Confession: I do, sometimes.

So, when it comes to putting pen to paper here, I would often rather write about traveling or adventure, and consider leaving the rest behind.

I've always been a place person. I love new sights and sounds and smells (thank you, 2006 pizza from Italy). However, as much as I consider myself a travel-bug, I'm now convinced, it's people, not places, that change you. Even if you're at home, in the same neighborhoods, day in and day out.

It's not about the sum total of all the places you've been. Monuments and new foods and scenery aren't what it's all about to me now, as much as these things are great.

I went to Colorado last year. It was a vacation/conference so I got myself together to go, to leave work finally after not taking a vacation in a few years. I had visions of mountain climbing and seeing all the beautiful sights. I ended up sick as a dog and in one of the worst forest fires they've had. What did I remember? The family of ten I stayed with who put me up and cared for me when I was down and out, the people I met who I near-evacuated the city with, a mentor/friend who I finally got to meet face-to-face on the day the fires broke out (we had a fireside chat).

I still had a wonderful time. It didn't matter that I didn't see the mountains up close. It mattered that I saw people up close. It's people who give rise to the adventures we remember.

You might have been to 30 places; I might have been to one. You might have gone everywhere; I might have stayed back every time. Both are good, both are needed. Both tales of traveling. Every day, my travels include visiting homes in my local town, and it is worth sharing.

Author: Julie LaJoe

I believe life is good and worth living to the full. I am learning to see beauty and grace in the everyday. I love Jesus and people and where the two intersect. I like to write about these things.

MercyNotes.com

A Life Defined

I've given a lot of thought to the piece I would write for this cause. I love the idea of Couch Rebels; and using my writing as a way to contribute to charity is something I've been striving for. But I struggled to come up with an idea worthy of this topic.

My life is simple. I haven't traveled abroad with a nonprofit charity or hiked through uncharted land. You see, I have late-stage, chronic Lyme disease, along with a bucket full of other 'chronic' labels and neurological complications. For the past decade or so, I've spent the majority of my time inside my own home. So what have I done in my life that has put me outside my comfort zone?

As I mulled this question over, the answer came with sudden clarity: pretty much everything. I am and always have been a full-fledged introvert. Being an introvert in an extrovert-oriented world means I stretch the boundaries of my comfort zone on a regular basis. On top of my introverted nature, I suffer from sensory overload. This is a neurological complication caused by the Lyme, and means excess stimulation - bright lights, crowds, lots of noise - causes my brain to short circuit. The result can be anything from mild confusion and vision disturbance to extreme disorientation, agitation, and blurred vision. All this put together means the simple act of going to the mall takes me out of my comfort zone.

Still, that's not a story worth telling. My health challenges don't make for fascinating reading. However, this all leads up to a story I hope is at least interesting.

Back in the late '90s, my health deteriorated to the point where I had to stop working. I needed something productive to do with my time, so I joined an online support group for people with chronic health problems. I didn't join to talk about myself, because I don't like to do that. (Which is yet another way I am now stepping out of my comfort zone.) I joined as a moderator, to listen to others, offer support, and provide information when possible. From there, I quickly became a contributor to the site's library, writing articles on various illnesses and treatments.

In this support group, I met a woman who was suffering with a variety of complications. She was about my age and lived on the other side of the country. We became friends, talking often on both the site's chat program and the telephone. Months later, her doctor referred her to a medical center in Colorado for a battery of tests. Since she lived in Nevada, she'd have to stay in a hotel near the hospital for one week. She asked if I would accompany her. Because I knew a lot about the medical world, she wanted me there to help her and also to ask all the questions she didn't think of.

I'd never met her in person. I'd never gone off for a week on my own. I definitely wasn't comfortable being even semi-responsible for someone else's healthcare.

I said yes.

I first flew to her home in Reno, Nevada, where I got to spend a couple of days playing tourist. From there, it was off to Colorado together.

I spent the week

accompanying her to all her tests and meetings with various doctors, taking notes, asking questions, and offering her emotional support. My own health took a beating that week. I did far more than I should have, and was both physically and emotionally drained. This woman turned out to be the type who needed - craved - constant attention. She also didn't push herself in the least. Her sickness became her license to sit back and let the world take care of her.

By the end of that week, this woman grated on my nerves in a spectacular way. Even so, I felt sorry for her. She used her illness like a crutch. She played up her health problems to elicit sympathy. In her desperation to keep people close to her, she wound up pushing them all away.

Despite the difficulties of that week, I wouldn't change a thing. I learned a lot about myself. I'm more resilient than I often give myself credit for. And I'm capable of taking care of myself, despite the obstacles my health problems toss in my way. More importantly, I am not and never will be defined by my illness.

Author: Darcia Helle

Suspense, random blood splatter, and mismatched socks consume Darcia Helle's days. She writes because the characters trespassing through her mind leave her no alternative.

QuietFuryBooks.com

On Destitute Teens and Barbies

I know a teenager who is destitute.

The same girl steals. Of course she does. That's what happens when you lack everything.

So when it came time to divvy extra Christmas cash, this girl did not make the cut. While others offered up her name, I shook my head.

Tsk. Tsk.

Hope is big and grace grand, but a thief?

Seriously, you expect me to give to a thief?

You've heard the stories about the drugs and the family drama and the jail time, right?

Suckers.

And then it happened; I saw her mother. Sure, I've seen her mom many times, but this time I saw her mother. The mother was standing on the side of the road with a blanket of goods stretched out before her: a couple of still packaged Barbies, neatly folded piles of clothes, and a baby doll stroller.

It was 31 degrees and the sky which threatened all day, finally started to sputter snow, but instead of snow falling, my own self-righteousness crashed straight through the roof of my perfectly heated car.

Instantly, poverty had a face, and it was the face of a person selling trinkets and tidbits from her house in the snow on the side of the road.

Instantly, poverty had a face, and it was the face of a person selling trinkets and tidbits from her house in the snow on the side of the road.

~ Amy L. Sullivan

www.bibledude.net

I wondered if the Barbies once belonged to the teenage girl. If as a little girl, she dreamed of brushing each doll's perfectly styled hair. I imagined the girl's mother telling her to leave the dolls in the box and that maybe one day her dolls would be worth some money.

One day.

Author: Amy Sullivan

Amy L. Sullivan is selfish, selfish, selfish, but for the past two years she's pretended not to be.

AmyLSullivan1.com

Discovered in a Skein of Yarn: Life Defining Lesson

I was 5 months pregnant. My nesting instinct was raging. It made me want to do unexpected things. I created a baby and apparently this baby was going to change my life. First she took over my womb. Then she made me want to do things I never expected to do. Like knit.

With a round belly I waddled into the local knitting store and meekly asked "do you have classes?" My intent was to gather information. I walked out with a receipt that said "$40" on paper but said "life defining moment" in my heart.

The moment I declared, "I want to knit" I simultaneously realized, "this baby is going to teach me things I never imagined I could learn."

I was stepping into a world that blends creativity and math – two of my least favorite things. Why in the world would I want to start a new hobby – one that I certainly wouldn't like, and couldn't do – just months before having a baby? My nesting instinct didn't offer me a choice. It demanded I fulfill this need my baby created.

Before she was even born, Marlee pushed me out of my comfort zone into an unknown world.

Learning to knit was akin to learning to become a parent.

I learned to knit one stitch at a time. I learned to parent one step at a time. With both, I learn from my mistakes and move forward.

Knitting taught me an important life lesson: be present.

I walked out of my last class with a project: a baby blanket. I was positive it would be my first and last project. But with each stitch I gained confidence. I became more patient. I could see the results of my hard work right in my hands.

The same applies to being a mom. Each day my confidence grows. My patience expands. I see my effort blossom before my eyes in the form of two kind, creative, funny children, of whom I am in awe.

I sat on my couch for hours knitting that baby blanket. I was immersed in the moment – I was soothed by the way the yarn felt in my fingers and the sound of the needles clinking together. I couldn't put the blanket down. I knit for hours.

When Marlee was born I was captivated by the softness of her skin and riveted by every sound she made. I was immersed in the moment. I was simultaneously terrified at this awesome responsibility and amazed that I was her mom. I held her tight for hours.

I finished the blanket but I wasn't done knitting. I went to the yarn store and started a new project. When finished, the hat had a point on the top, but I proudly put it on Marlee's head every day.

My girls regularly shine a bright, glaring light on all the parenting skills I have yet to learn. I learn as I go, hoping to gain the knowledge needed to be the parent they each deserve.

My friend Jen once told me, "You don't need to know everything at once. You just need to be one step ahead of your child." I reflect on this each time I fall into despair that perhaps I am not fit to be a mom.

Like the time I briefly let go of the shopping cart and a strong wind whisked Marlee just out of my reach. A woman was shrieking nearby as I watched Marlee race across the parking lot. The woman and countless other bystanders were paralyzed. I had the presence of mind to visualize the best possible outcome. I willed a van to move between her and the main road to stop the cart.

The scene unfolded exactly as I envisioned it. The van stopped the shopping cart just as I approached. Marlee flew into the air and I caught her. I was 3 months pregnant with my next child. This incident crippled my confidence and made me wonder how I could possibly be a mom to one child, let alone two.

I realized that knitting has taught me to visualize outcomes. It requires me to create a picture of my project in my mind. The same approach applied to the parking lot incident. I use it daily as a mom. I visualize the outcome. I imagine how it will feel when the picture becomes reality.

Despite my natural tendency to think in absolute terms, I am now inspired to think differently and find many ways to tackle a challenge..with knitting, with parenting, in life.

Before Marlee arrived, my friend Jamie asked me if I was excited. I admitted that I was terrified…of everything. He explained, "This is the beginning of a lifetime of being terrified. It all starts when your baby is born." His words were so candid and so true that I was instantly ready to be a mom.

When my nesting instinct insisted that I learn to knit I had no idea it would become a passion. How could something I never intended to do become something I couldn't wait to do?

When I first met Josh I declared "I never want to have kids". Yet here I am 21 years later with more love in my heart than I could have ever imagined. Something I was sure I never wanted has become the thing I can't live without.

Knitting taught me to be fully present.

Becoming a mom gave me a reason to want to experience every moment.

And while stepping outside my comfort zone is supposed to get me OFF the couch, learning to knit prepared me to spend more time ON my couch, where I cuddle and bond with my babies and my husband, where I learned to swap To-Do lists and carefully made plans for living in the moment. On my couch with my family and my knitting I am surrounded by love. I am free. And I am filled with joy.

Author: Jill Shaul

Jill Shaul is a mom, knitter, personal growth coach, communication specialist and much, much more. She is likely sitting on her couch with her family, a knitting project, and a half-written blog.

JillShaul.com

When I Grow Up I Want to Be...

On January 23, 2009, my life changed forever. I was 18.5 weeks pregnant with our third child and my husband, two kids, and I were going to find out if we were having a little brother or a little sister. It was a happy and exciting day for all of us, one we had been counting down to for weeks!

Having already gone through this two other times, I wasn't the least bit nervous. Hey, after two successful pregnancies and six years of motherhood, I was an expert! What could possibly go wrong?

"It's a BOY!" announced the ultrasound technician.

We were all thrilled! We already had his name picked out and we started to text our friends and family as the technician left the room.

Unbeknownst to us, the technician had called the high-risk obstetrician when she left the room. When Dr. Singh finally came in, he spent a few minutes looking at the ultrasound monitor and made a sound I never in my wildest dreams expected.

"Oh...Hmmm... do you see that mark right there on his face? That is a cleft lip. Do you know what that is?"

I knew what a cleft lip was but Dr. Singh launched into his explanation anyway. My husband and I just looked at each other, and for as long as I live, I will never forget what Dr. Singh did next. He held my hand, looked me in the eye, and said in the most solemn voice: "I'm so so sorry, I'm so sorry."

"There's nothing else wrong, right?" I begged. "It's just a cleft and can be fixed, right?"

"As far as I can tell, everything else looks completely normal" He responded. "But I would like you to have an MRI done in Boston to see if there is anything else going on. My staff will help you book appointments in Boston..."

My head was heavy and spinning. My ears, blocked. I could hear him talking but couldn't focus on anything else he was saying. I wanted to run. How could this happen? What did I do wrong? Why was Dr. Singh SO incredibly sad? Is this how everyone is going to treat my baby?

The weekend that followed the ultrasound was one of the most difficult of my life. I spent too much time researching cleft lip, cleft palate, chromosomal abnormalities and all kinds of syndromes I didn't even know existed. I couldn't get Dr. Singh's reaction out of my head. I kept hearing his voice: "I'm so so sorry, I'm so sorry."

I was supposed to attend a baby shower that Sunday. I woke up Sunday from a night of broken sleep and couldn't get out of bed. I did not want to go to a baby shower and celebrate someone else's perfect baby when I was terrified for my own baby. I just couldn't do it.

Only... I did do it.

I got out of that bed. I stood up. I got dressed. I washed my tear-soaked face, texted my sister and told her I was coming. I put on a brave face, put one foot in front of the other, and walked into that baby shower to celebrate the joy that comes with all new babies.

I was very visibly pregnant and many people at the shower asked me about the baby. Somehow, someway, I was able to talk about it like the Friday appointment never happened. I was able to just feel happy, without letting the dread and worry set in. Just, happy. Happy like I had felt for the previous 14 weeks. For the first time since Friday morning, I started to feel like maybe everything was going to be okay.

Four long weeks later, I had an MRI in Boston which confirmed a complete unilateral cleft lip and palate. We met with our surgical team at Boston Children's Hospital and reviewed what our son's first year of life would be like.

The rest of my pregnancy wasn't easy. I ran through a gamut of emotions. I continued to research (damn the Internet!) and had days where I was completely fine, and days where I was more than a little bit crazy. I cried. I was angry. I worried that I had ruined my other two kids' lives. I worried I wasn't a good enough parent; wasn't strong enough to handle this. I have always heard "God doesn't give you more than you can handle" but I wasn't sure. This was maybe more than I could handle. I knew the first year of his life was going to be the hardest year of mine.
Some say that babies choose their parents. What if he chose wrong?

Every time I asked my husband that question, he pointed to our bedroom wall. On our wall hangs one of my daughter's preschool projects, dated January 22, 2009. She wasn't yet 4 years old when, on the day before our first ultrasound, her preschool teacher posed the question to her students: When I Grow Up I Want to Be _____.

My daughter's answer, in beautiful, shaky preschool handwriting was: "MOMMY"

I started to tell myself maybe he didn't choose wrong after all.

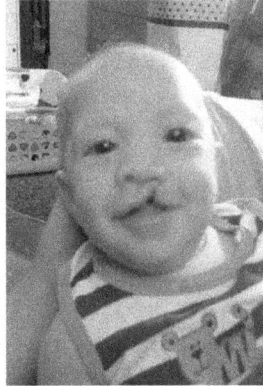

After a very short labor, Mason James was born at 6:25 a.m. on June 4, 2009. As the nurse laid him in my arms and I gazed into his sweet little face for the first time, I swear I didn't see a cleft. I didn't see a birth defect. I just didn't see it. I kissed him and all I saw was perfect beauty. All those months of worry, fear, and self-doubt, all washed away in an instant.

"You're finally here" were my first words to my new son.

And just like that, I knew I wouldn't have any trouble getting out of bed anymore. I knew we'd get through this. I knew I would be the mother my son needed me to be.

Author: Kim Phillips

Kim Phillips is a writer, mother, wife, sister, daughter, auntie, cousin and friend. She has enjoyed creative writing since the third grade and writing in a professional business setting since 1996.

Thepichronicles.blogspot.com

The Little Ministry That Could

Thinking back to the first time I heard about Operation Christmas Child, it was such a small conversation, but one that lead to a new little mission project for our church. One never knows how words can change a person's future or heart, in this case mine. This little conversation ended up changing my life and our church forever.

That first year, the only thing I knew was that the gifts were for suffering children overseas. Images of pot-bellied children who didn't have enough energy to shoo a fly floated through my mind. Heart strings pulled, I shopped for the items to go into our boxes. Thinking about the girl that would get our box, I could almost see the smiles and hear the giggles that the small bright red etch-a-sketch would bring as she turned the knobs and watched the lines go everywhere. Memories of my child-like wonder at seeing a metal slinky work for the first time made me want to find room for one in that small container. Even finding just the right notebook and pencils was an exciting event. That first year our church collected just fifteen shoeboxes, but for a church of sixty and a ladies group of fifteen, that wasn't too bad.

The next year, things started to change in our church. One of the ladies in our group, Annette, explained Operation Christmas Child to two of her best friends, Betty Lou and Marie. By godly coincidence, Marie owned a dollar store. Marie and Betty Lou were so touched by the stories of the children that they would have raffles at the store to raise money for the cause. With the extra help we filled eighty-six shoeboxes.

Our church has continued to increase the number of shoeboxes each year by leaps and bounds. Packaging as many shoeboxes as our church does requires super shoppers. Don't expect to find a pencil, sharpener, or notebook on tax free weekend at any store around. Marie also helps a lot by selling us many items at cost from her store. Yard sales and selling food boxes are all part of the fundraising and the fun.

Even though our church collectively does the bulk of the shoeboxes, I still like to make my own. I do find things on sale, though I am not one of the super shoppers. Any extra money also goes to this ministry. There is something about praying for the child that will get my box and feeling God's leading as to what to put in the boxes that makes it so much more meaningful. Picking just the right colored hair bow, the right coloring book and of course the flip flops. Every box needs flip flops. I find it so heartbreaking to know that these kids don't even have shoes. If they don't have shoes, then most of them can't go to school.

I started hearing the testimonies from the "frontlines" of giving out the shoeboxes in the publicity packets. There have been several that really touched me, but the one where the little boy received a shoebox full of socks, no candy or toys, moved me the most. The person giving out the boxes felt bad for the child and tried to exchange it with another box. The boy was so happy with his box; he wouldn't let the box go. This reaction was so confusing to the worker that she asked the teacher. It turns out that the boy was in a bad fire which left his legs scarred from burns. The kids would tease him about his scars. God had taken care of that for him with the socks.

After a few years our church had grown to over eight hundred shoeboxes. Now it was a full blown year round church wide ministry project. Other churches in the area were now participating, which lead the association to plan to go to work at the distribution center. Of course I had to sign up. There was so much to learn: take out the liquids, breakables, candy that melts, and war related items; take out the money for shipping; put the items back in; and tape the box back up. I found the hardest job was putting the items back in. Most of the creators of these boxes know how to over pack.

There have been many more heart tugging front-line testimonies, which engrained in me the realization that I don't have to go across the world to do God's work. It can be accomplished in my own backyard with a fun project. I came back from that mission trip energized, but tired to the bone.

Last year, during my trip to the distribution center, I started seeing expensive tools in the boxes. I was confused, not knowing exactly if I should keep those in the boxes. The hammers, screwdrivers and wrenches were adult items, but I felt like God wanted them to stay in as the creators of the boxes wanted. Later I heard testimonies of kids getting hammers and screwdrivers. They were so excited because now their families could earn some money. How good is our God!

This past year, our church of around sixty created over two thousand shoeboxes. We have the processes all worked out. The super shoppers shop, the organizers organize and count the items in bins by type, the baggers bag up small bags of candy and soap. These activities are done all year. At the appropriate month, the process line starts. Working this ministry has changed my life, and our church's life. Hopefully, we are changing the lives of children across the world, one shoebox at a time. Only God could prompt a little country church to this ministry, to grow it into the massive year long ministry project that it has become. Thank you Jesus.

Author: Carla Rogers

I love finding ways to serve God within my day to day activities. I am also getting good at taking a leap of faith. I am a wife and hopefully at some point a mother to an adoptive child.

Indian Intervention

The past does not determine our future, it's only a shadow of what's to come. Two years ago I read a book about the street children in India, and my heart for the country grew. I had a heart for the less fortunate and had been on several short term missions trips over the years, but did not feel led to go anywhere long term. This was different, I had a heart for a country that I hadn't ever been to and could not explain the pull towards it. This had to be a God thing, but how on earth was God going to speak to me now of all times? I wasn't even living for Him, battling a deep depression, crying myself to sleep every night, and miserable. I didn't know which end was up, and God still wanted to use me? I was humbled after I read the book, but I needed something more, I needed the joy that I knew can only come from the Lord, and I needed purpose! In complete desperation crying out to Him, I asked Him to take control and show me my next steps.

I looked into several organizations that might help me get to India, but nothing clicked. I put that desire on a shelf and trucked on with life. At the time I was working for Cruella De-Vil at a fashion house as an assistant designer, and knew my contract was coming to a close. I couldn't wait to high tail it out of there and move near my family again. I had been away from them for seven years, and with a job offer on the table I jumped at the chance. The only difference in this move versus the past seven years of my life was that I prayed about it! I knew that this was my next step, and that my path would be blessed.

Going back home wasn't easy in the beginning, as I faced a past I wasn't comfortable with, and a family structure I didn't know how to function in anymore. Life does go on when you move away, who knew?! It took a few months to settle in, as I spent time with my family and learned the ins and outs of my new job. I can't tell you how refreshing it was to work for somebody so life giving and edifying. Sometimes it isn't what you are doing for a living, it is who you are doing it with that makes all the difference in the world. Six months into working for this amazing company I learned that our investment capital was waning, and they wouldn't be able to keep me on for salary. Wait a second here, hold on! What? I thought God had brought me here, I thought this was the move He wanted me to make and that this path would be blessed? Once again, what is my purpose?

Deep down I knew that everything would be ok, and a few short months into my unemployment, life jumped into overdrive. It happened to be my thirty-first birthday and some of my dearest friends kidnapped me for a pampering day. I needed it too, I didn't want to slink back into my lazy self-consumed state of depressed oblivion. I had overcome so much since I had been home, including kicking my anti-depressants to the curb, and being so full of joy I barely recognized myself. It's one thing to say you're happy, and another to truly feel joy! As all of us girls were getting our nails done, my friend leaned over and said, "Hey, our Pastor mentioned that there is an opportunity to go to India, and you came to all of our minds, would you have any desire to go?" Deep breath in, deep breath out, YES!

I couldn't believe that those words had come out of her mouth. I could have jumped out of my skin with excitement. Moreover, she said the church was covering all expenses and would be sending me. It had been two years since I heard that I was supposed to go, but I hadn't thought about it since then. So many promises from the Bible started running through my head. If He starts a good work in you, He will see it through to completion. He has plans to prosper and not to harm you, and so forth. You see the Lord's Word never falls void and when He puts in you a dream or desire He will always see it through to completion.

Today I am currently in India working in an orphanage, loving on those less fortunate than myself. I have been here for a month now, and God has given me a vision so beyond myself that I know it's His work within me. In the very near future I will be starting a rehabilitation center for women rescued from the sex trade industry. I know this endeavor won't be an easy road, but God says His yoke is easy and His burdens are light, and I won't be doing it alone. I have the Lord as my guide, and what an amazing guide He is. If He can take my used and abused soul and fill me with the joy I'm filled with today, I know anything is possible.

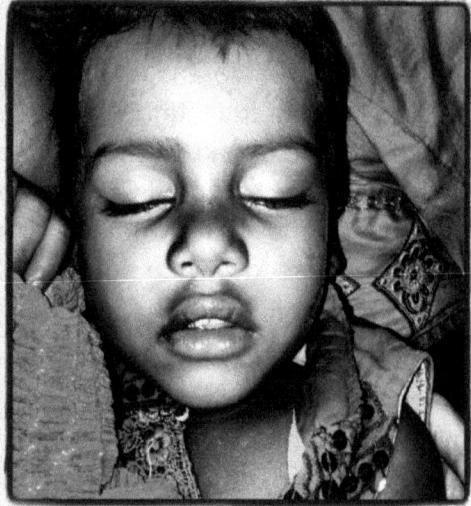

Life is an adventure and we only have one chance to live it! It took me some time to get to where I am, but now that I'm here there is no turning back! I couldn't see the purpose in my past experiences until now. Each journey I went through led to this one. Often God's timing is not our own, live in the moment, because your time is coming! We each have a story that is written in its own time, in its own language, and every book is a page turner to the right reader. Thank you Lord for writing my story!

Author: Lauren Yeager

Lover of people, excited about Jesus, purposed for greatness, fashion enthusiast, world traveler, and philanthropic fanatic. I love the perfectly flawed! Currently in India working in an orphanage.

ThisIsMyPlatform.blogspot.com

Contrast

On Wednesday evenings people occupy spaces in a dimly lit sanctuary. They gather around tables where votive candles flicker with light. Napkins hold rows of cookies and heat rises from mugs of hot chocolate.

I have never crossed an ocean. But I have walked four blocks from my home, deep into the neighborhood I live. In this Midwest town a church resides on every corner and tulip rows line the streets. Across the sidewalk squares of town are also lines of graffiti, gang symbols etched into the playground equipment, and poverty.

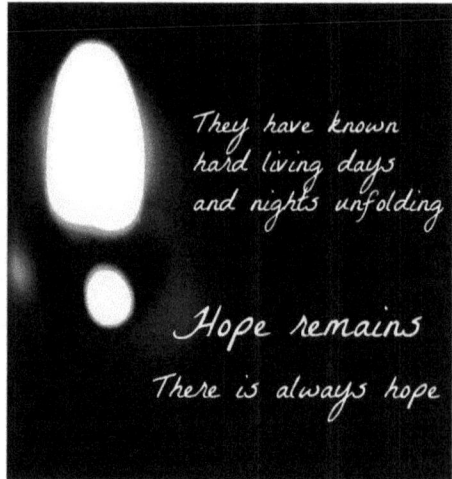

They have known hard living days and nights unfolding

Hope remains

There is always hope

They sleep on beds provided by the rescue mission. Some have waited in winding lines for food. Mental illness seeps through minds and plagues heartbeats. Sometimes one will stumble to the table in an altered mental state of addiction. The metal bars of imprisonment have encircled. For some, mental disability does not slow the trajectory of their lives.

Histories of hurt gather up strength and push to the present. They have known hard living days and nights unfolding again and again. In small offerings of prayer they speak of their lives made up of vulnerable threads.

They pray for mission beds at winter capacity. Another person cries out a prayer that children don't know the pain they did as a child living with hunger. For a young single mother in an empty apartment, can they gather their own sparse belongings so she has enough? Can someone accompany a father who will visit a son in a juvenile detention center? One disabled friend speaks for another who cannot form the correct words. A dire health situation, yes we will walk with you in the morning. A ride to an appointment, I will take you.

Lives pressed into ashes, covered over in forgiveness. They rise to hold a hand, wrap an arm around another, offer an embrace, gather a chair for a straggler and shake the hand of an elderly visitor. The contrast in the color of their skin does not matter.

No one speaks in solitude. One voice sounds, then a phrase is added, another voice turning; their words piece together to form something whole.

In mercy, scraps of brokenness form beauty when placed together.

All pride seeps from my heart during that hour. I sit in a chair pressed against the chair of a mentally disabled friend. She likes for me to keep my arm around her during the study. Words don't leave my mouth. Their words and actions are far more eloquent than my small offerings. I sit with them in their brokenness and their fractured prayers. Though I have not known their heartache, I can offer my presence as one of them, a broken person in need of hope.

Hope remains. There is always hope in a community willing to be broken together.

Author: Lisa Van Engen

I am a freelance writer that seeks to offer encouragement.

AboutProximity.com

What's *Your* Couch Rebel Story?

Get up.

Go find it.

Want to participate in a book project?

CausePub.com

List of Authors

(Listed in the same order as how the stories appear in the book. Authors who wrote two stories may be listed twice.)

- Griff Hanning (organizer/editor)
- Ashleigh Slater
- Lori Harris
- Brandy Campbell
- Jay Sanders
- Chris Morris
- Melissa Aldrich
- Katie Cross
- Elizabeth Meinster
- Drew Tilton
- Stephanie Hoffer
- Abby Andrus
- Jenny Price
- Jennifer Camp
- Maury McCown
- Don Wilks
- Dana Rausch
- Hannah Rose Allen
- Jillian Amodio
- Michelle Hanning
- Melissa Tenpas
- Joshua McNeal
- Sarah Siders
- Shelly Miller
- Stephanie Page
- Amber Lia
- Sarah Ray

- Kari Day
- Cindy Cooper
- Rachael McKinney
- Brandee Shafer
- Beth Stiff
- Dallas Owen
- Leah Morford
- Carol Hatcher
- Beth Coulton
- Jaime Lind
- Marc Sandin
- Joanne Viola
- Aidan DeMuth
- Jenny Price
- Suzanne Gosselin
- Danielle Christy
- Beck Gambill
- Kaitlin Clark
- Ingrid Jansons
- Mike Lenda
- Greg Coles
- Stephanie Page
- Ian Anderson
- Bethany Turner
- Karen McCown
- Rebecca Kinabrew
- Jen Lewis
- Brian Gensch
- Eileen Knowles
- Matt Ehresman
- Rebecca VanDeMark

- Kay Bruner
- Jessica Naramore
- Megan McDonald
- Gaby Johnson
- Tara Lakes
- Karin Hume
- Melissa Tenpas
- Jim Burmeister
- Mel Schroeder
- Dallas Owen
- Becca Marsh
- Austin Mann
- Chelsea Mills
- Beck Gambill
- Lauren Monitz
- Jennifer Camp
- Alex Beaverson
- Rebecca VanDeMark
- Olivia Fulmer
- Jeni Mason
- Mandy Scarr
- Julie LaJoe
- Darcia Helle
- Amy Sullivan
- Jill Shaul
- Kim Phillips
- Carla Rogers
- Lauren Yeager
- Lisa Van Engen